DATE DUE

About the author

John M. Swomley, Jr., is professor of Christian
Social Ethics and Philosophy of Religion at the
St. Paul School of Theology in Kansas City, Mis-
souri. Nationally known through his activities in
the peace movement, he lectures frequently on
questions of the individual's relation to the state.
He is author of *The Military Establishment* (1964),
and his articles have appeared in *The Christian
Century, Fellowship,* and *The Christian Advocate.*
He is vice-president of the Western Missouri Civil
Liberties Union, and chairman of its Church-State
Committee, and is a member of the Committee on
Civil and Religious Liberty of the National Coun-
cil of Churches.

JOHN M. SWOMLEY, JR.

RELIGION, THE STATE & THE SCHOOLS

Pegasus • New York

ACKNOWLEDGMENTS

Acknowledgment is gratefully made to the following authors and publishers for permission to quote from previously published works:

Emil Brunner, *The Divine Imperative*, trans. by Olive Wyon. Copyright 1947 by W. K. Jenkins. Reprinted by permission from The Westminster Press.

The Catholic Layman, July, 1963. Reprinted by permission from The Paulist Press, Glen Rock, New Jersey.

The Catholic Reporter of April 31, 1964, Apr. 2, 1965, and January 20, 1967. Reprinted by permission of *The New People*, successor to *The Catholic Reporter*, Kansas City, Missouri.

Arthur Hertzberg, "Church, State and the Jews," quoted from *Commentary* by permission. Copyright © 1963 by the American Jewish Committee.

Marvin Karpatkin, letter to the editor of *America*, Apr. 9, 1966. Reprinted by permission of *America*, The National Catholic Weekly Review, 106 West 56th St., New York, N.Y. 10019. © 1966, America Press, Inc.

The Reverend John Courtney Murray, "Governmental Repression of Heresy". Quoted from *Proceedings of the Catholic Theological Society of America, III*, June 1949, by permission.

Mary Perkins Ryan, *Are Parochial Schools the Answer?* Copyright 1964 by Mary Perkins Ryan. Reprinted by permission from Holt, Rinehart & Winston, Inc., publishers.

The Reverends John A. Ryan and Francis J. Boland, *Catholic Principles of Politics: The State and the Church*. Copyright 1940 by the National Catholic Welfare Conference; tenth printing 1960. Reprinted by permission from The Macmillan Company, publisher, New York, N.Y.

Peter H. and Alice S. Rossi, "Some Effects of Parochial School Education." Spring, 1961, *Daedulus*. Reprinted by permission from *Daedulus*. Copyright 1961, American Academy of Arts and Sciences, Boston, Massachusetts.

Edward Wakin, "How Catholic Is a Catholic College?" *Saturday Review*, Apr. 16, 1966; reprinted by permission.

To Katie

Congress shall make no law respecting an establishment of religion, or prohibiting the free exercise thereof; or abridging the freedom of speech or of the press; or the right of the people peaceably to assemble and to petition the Government for a redress of grievances.

—The First Amendment

Preface

For many years the American people have been involved in a Church–State controversy in the area of education. Protestant–Catholic rivalries were the fuel that fed the flames, and emotions confirmed each side in its position. As a result many Roman Catholics believe that opposition to government aid to parochial schools is simply Protestant bias. Many Protestants oppose such aid solely because it would be aid to the Roman Catholic Church. Other Protestants often favor such aid if only to prove their general tolerance and lack of bias. Regrettably, the rational basis for the controversy tends to be overlooked in each of these positions, and it is the intention of this volume to discuss the full dimensions of the several issues involved.

The current debates and struggles over the relationship of religion, the state and the schools are historically rooted in centuries of European and American experience and are manifest in a number of recent changes, not always related to education. For example, the question of aid to church schools is not simply a question of educational policy, since it is vitally affected both by

Protestant, Roman Catholic and Jewish interpretations of religious liberty and by the political philosophy of the courts and legislators. In order adequately to deal with the historical character of the problems, this book is divided into two major sections. The first deals briefly with the development of the current Church–State context. The second analyzes the specific ways in which present religious, educational and governmental interests intersect. In conclusion a series of proposals are made concerning governmental involvement with religion in education.

In the process of writing and editing this book I have discovered how markedly my own thinking and that of most of the major Protestant denominations have changed concerning the proper relationship of the conflicting interests of Church and State. A powerful impetus for change was the spirit of Vatican II, which to some degree eliminated the old cloying Protestant fear of a privileged Roman Catholic educational establishment. But, including Vatican II, two developments in particular have radically changed the direction and nature of my thought—specifically the work of civil libertarians and that of progressive Catholics. The civil libertarians and their allies the humanists and the Jews have taught me to abhor equally the dangers of a present Protestant establishment as being as destructive of liberties as possible Catholic privilege. Of equal importance is their warning against a religious secularism, often nationalistic in character, whose appeal is based on the lowest-common-denominator claims of faith.

The remarkable development of the ecumenical spirit within the Roman Catholic Church has had a profound effect on those Protestants, myself among them, who had feared the social and educational objectives of the Roman hierarchy. Some of the most vigorous voices within the Church now claim that by seeking active governmental support of the parochial school, the school is falsely perpetuated as the center of parish life, diverting the Church from its primary ministry to the poor and sick and from its work for the elimination of the social conditions that breed poverty and war.

John Cogley, a Roman Catholic layman, stated this point of view in *The New People*, August 25, 1967, when he called parochial schools "a massive diversion from the apostolic and pastoral mission of the Church." He added: "The problem is that we are stuck . . . with buildings, ancient commitments, a misguided tradition, and a pre-modern concept that the Church should handle the total educational job instead of its proper share of it."

The effect of such claims by both clergy and laity points up the failure of the institutionalists, in the Roman as well as the Protestant Church, to represent the whole Church and to recognize that they may, in fact, be the Church's unintentional enemies. It is highly probable that those who oppose state aid to parochial schools may be more helpful to both Catholic and Protestant Church interests than those who favor such aid. The issue however is "religious" and not parochial, since fear of Catholic privilege is duplicated by distrust of Protestant college and hospital administrators who are in continuing search for governmental aid. An unacknowledged alliance of Protestant and Catholic ecclesiasts could drastically alter our understanding of the religious liberties and the right of all men to the freedom of conscience.

The issue then is not limited to the Roman Church, although in the chapters that follow, particular attention will be paid to the efforts of the Roman hierarchy and to the lay organization Citizens for Educational Freedom. Equal emphasis will be given the less publicized activity of Protestant college and hospital administrators as well as other Protestant efforts to establish religious observances in the public schools.

The concern of the writer is to present the entire problem with objectivity while making his own claim for the total separation of all Church activities from governmental support. In all that follows, the presentation is not intended to indict persons or churches but to analyze claims, strategies and trends in the hope that the avoidance of any religious establishment will result in broader civil and religious liberties and a more effective church.

I wish to thank Gaston Cogsdell and Dean M. Kelley, who read this book in manuscript form. Their suggestions were very helpful, although they are not, of course, to be held responsible for the contents. Above all, I am grateful for the typing and other assistance of my wife Marjie.

JOHN M. SWOMLEY
OCTOBER 31, 1967

Contents

RELIGION,
THE STATE
&
THE SCHOOLS

PART I

The Current Church–State Context

1

The Constitutional Context

"Congress shall make no law respecting an establishment of religion or prohibiting the free exercise thereof." These sixteen words in the First Amendment to the United States Constitution are the basis for the unique American idea of separation of Church and State. The concept of separation did not come from the political traditions of the European countries, which had established churches and which, with the exception of Holland, could not be described as havens for religious dissenters. Many of the original Colonies, however, also had established churches and restrictions on religious liberty and the First Amendment was adopted only after successful demonstrations and struggle had paved the way. The demonstrations occurred in Rhode Island and Pennsylvania, where there was a high degree of religious freedom and no established church, but the early struggle for disestablishment occurred in Virginia under the able leadership of James Madison. In each of these states the opposition to established churches was in part the product of the activity of religious groups. The Quakers played a major role in Pennsylvania, and the

Baptists, under Roger Williams' leadership, in Rhode Island. In Virginia both Baptists and Presbyterians were influential.

Another major ideological influence was the philosophy of John Locke, the popularizer of the social contract theory of government. Locke asserted in his first *Letter Concerning Toleration* that "the care of souls cannot belong to the civil magistrate because his power consists only in outward force; but true and saving religion consists in the inward persuasion of the mind. . . ."[1] Locke had been a dominating influence on many leading Americans, including Jefferson and Madison. Partly under his influence, they came to believe that a government that was formed as a social contract had no power given to it to act on religious matters.

A number of the political leaders following the Revolution were both deists and rationalists and therefore not eager to provide governmental support to orthodox churches. They were not alone in their feeling about the churches, for during the post-revolutionary period the overwhelming majority of Americans were not church members. Those who were churchmen were divided, since the nonestablished or free churches tended to oppose special status for the established churches—hence opposing the principle of establishment. The deists and the unchurched were not politically hostile to religion; they looked upon it as a matter of private decision. Only if it was private could the more important values of freedom of conscience and dissent be safeguarded.

It was in Virginia that the decisive struggle for separation of Church and State occurred. The Anglican Church in that state was established, but there were more members of such dissenting churches as the Baptists and Presbyterians. When the Virginia Convention in 1776 adopted the Bill of Rights for the state constitution, it agreed that "all men are equally entitled to the free exercise of religion. . . ." The "free exercise" statement did not, however, end establishment or taxation for the established church. The Baptists, Presbyterians and others then petitioned the legislature to abolish establishment. The legislature, which was controlled in December, 1776, by churchmen, repealed certain laws regarding the established church, thereby providing that dissenters did not have to pay taxes for its support, but it left open the possibility of taxation for the support of the church of each man's choice. The issue was finally joined when Patrick Henry sponsored a Bill Establishing a Provision for Teachers of the Christian Religion, which would have required everyone to pay an annual tax "for he support of the Christian religion, or of some Christian church. . . ."[2] In effect, all Christian churches, including the dissenting sects, would have become established. James Madison, who led the opposition, wrote the now famous "Memorial and Remonstrance Against Religious Assessments." In one of his fifteen arguments, he asserted:

> *The same authority which can establish Christianity, in exclusion of all other religions, may establish with the same ease any particular sect of Christians in exclusion of all other sects, and the same authority which can force a citizen to contribute three pence only of his property for the support of any one establishment, may force him to conform to any other establishment in all cases whatsoever.*[3]

Madison's position prevailed as a result of a combination of events, including the election of Patrick Henry as governor, his consequent departure from the legislature and the wide support from most religious groups and geographical areas of the state. After the defeat of the assessment bill, Madison and his supporters in 1786 secured the passage of Jefferson's earlier Bill for Establishing Religious Freedom, which had failed to pass when first introduced in the legislature in 1779. The preamble to that statute points out that "it is sinful and tyrannical to compel a man to furnish contributions for the propagation of opinions which he disbelieves and abhors; and it is also wrong to force him to support this or that teacher of his own religious persuasion."[4]

Elected to the nation's House of Representatives, James Madison introduced in 1789 a proposed Bill of Rights, which was amended, adopted by the House and Senate and ratified in 1791 by the required number of states. The Virginia struggle over establishment, in which Madison played so decisive a role, thus had its carry-over into the First Amendment to the federal Constitution. Since the taxation of all for the benefit of all churches was the major issue in Virginia, it should be obvious that the

Constitution precludes the use of tax funds for religion, even if equitably distributed to all religious groups.

Today, a number of persons who believe that it is permissible for government to aid churches or church projects have made the point that the First Amendment applies only to Congress, thus leaving the President, the courts and the states free to do exactly what the First Amendment prohibits. One response to this made by such persons as Madison himself, historian Charles Beard and Leo Pfeffer, a leading constitutional lawyer, is that the federal government was never given any authority or jurisdiction over religion by the Constitution.[5] Charles Beard, for example, wrote: "The Constitution does not confer upon the federal government any power whatever to deal with religion in any form or manner."[6]

The Ninth Amendment quite clearly reaffirms what was implied from the beginning, that "the enumeration in the Constitution of certain rights shall not be construed to deny and disparage others retained by the people." A restriction imposed specifically on Congress, which initiates appropriations and adopts legislation, was not therefore to be construed as granting a power to the President or some other government agency. This is made clear in the Tenth Amendment, which states that "the powers not delegated to the United States by the Constitution, nor prohibited by it to the States, are reserved to the states respectively or to the people."

In view of the Tenth Amendment and the fact that some of the states continued to have an establishment of religion as late as 1833, it was clear that the First Amendment to the federal Constitution did not apply to the states. The Supreme Court, however, in 1947 in the Everson case, decided that the concept of separation of Church and State does apply to the states. It did so by invoking the Fourteenth Amendment to the Constitution. This amendment contains a clause that says: "No state shall make or enforce any law which shall abridge the privileges or immunities of citizens of the United States, nor shall any State deprive any person of life, liberty or property without due process of law. . . ." This section of the amendment was intended by Congress when it was adopted and sent to the states to make the first eight amendments of the Bill of Rights applicable to the states, although the Supreme Court has only gradually made these amendments applicable to the states.

In the congressional discussion of the proposed Fourteenth Amendment, Senator J. M. Howard (R.–Michigan), the amendment's floor manager, specifically stated in explaining it that "to these privileges and immunities . . . should be added the personal rights guaranteed and secured by the first eight amendments to the Constitution."[7] Senator Howard added, "The great object of the first section of the amendment is, therefore, to restrain the power of the states and compel them at all times to respect these fundamental guaranties."[8] In the House, Representative John Bingham (R.–Ohio), who was called by Justice Hugo Black "the Madison of the Fourteenth Amendment," also indicated that he intended that amendment to overthrow an earlier Supreme Court decision (*Barron vs. Baltimore*) that had held that the Bill of Rights was not applicable to the states.[9]

When in the Everson case the Supreme Court made the establishment clause of the First Amendment applicable to the states, the court also spelled out its meaning:

The "establishment of religion" clause of the First Amendment means at least this:

Neither a state nor the Federal Government can set up a church.

Neither can pass laws which aid one religion, aid all religions, or prefer one religion over another.

Neither can force nor influence a person to go to or to remain away from church against his will or force him to profess a belief or disbelief in any religion.

No person can be punished for entertaining or professing religious beliefs or disbeliefs, for church attendance or non-attendance.

No tax in any amount, large or small, can be levied to support any religious activities or institutions, whatever they may be called, or whatever form they may adopt to teach or practice religion.

Neither a state nor the Federal Government, can openly or secretly, participate in the affairs of any religious organization or groups and vice versa.

In the words of Jefferson, the clause against establishment of religion by law was intended to erect "a wall of separation between Church and State."[10]

Nevertheless, the concept of a wall did not provide a clear guideline on Church–State matters, as evident from the Everson decision itself. In *Everson* the court upheld by a 5–4 ruling the right of a state to reimburse the parents of public and private school children for the cost of transportation to and from school. Justice Black and four colleagues saw no breach of the wall, whereas Justice Wiley B. Rutledge and three other members of the court found that the wall was breached because in effect New Jersey subsidized religious education by relieving parents of the cost of transporting their children to church schools.

In 1948 in *McCollum vs. Board of Education,* the court decided that the arrangement was unconstitutional whereby public schools permitted children to be released for religious educational purposes on public school property under the compulsory attendance provisions. Justice Black held in his opinion that the State was not only using "tax supported public school buildings . . . for the dissemination of religious doctrines" but "the State also affords sectarian groups an invaluable aid in that it helps to provide pupils for their religious classes through use of the State's compulsory public school machinery. This is not separation of Church and State."[11] A few years later, In *Zorach vs. Clauson* (1952), the court permitted the release of pupils for religious classes off the premises of the public school, even though the compulsory attendance laws required the presence of those pupils whose parents did not request their release.[12] Clearly the wall did not mean exactly the same thing in *Zorach* as it did in *McCollum* or *Everson*.

Perhaps because the "wall of separation" was not fully adequate, the Supreme Court added to it the concept of "neutrality" in the 1963 decision in the Bible-reading and prayer cases (*Abington School District vs. Schempp* and *Murray vs. Curlett*). Justice Tom C. Clark wrote: "In the relationship between man and religion, the state is firmly committed to a position of neutrality. Though the application of that rule requires interpretation of a delicate sort, the rule itself is clearly and concisely stated in the words of the First Amendment."[13] Clark went on to indicate that "to withstand the strictures of the Establishment Clause there must be a secular legislative purpose and a primary effect that neither advances nor inhibits religion."[14]

The concept of neutrality is apparently conditioned by certain other considerations. Chief Justice Earl Warren suggested one in the case of *McGowan vs. Maryland*, which dealt with Sunday closing laws. Warren said that

> the *"Establishment"* clause does not ban federal or state regulation of conduct whose reason or effect merely happens to coincide or harmonize with the tenets of some or all religions. In many instances, the Congress or state legislatures conclude that the general welfare of society wholly apart from any religious considerations, demands such regulation.[15]

Warren, in other words, asserted that those Sunday laws which in effect aided certain religious groups had a purpose and effect that were primarily "secular" and thus were for the general welfare.

On the other hand, Justice William J. Brennan, in a concurring opinion in the Bible-reading and prayer cases, indicated that "the teaching of both *Torcaso* and the Sunday Law Cases is that government may not employ religious means to serve secular interests, however legitimate they may be, at least without the clearest demonstration that non-religious means will not suffice."[16]

Justice Brennan's statement is not the position of the court since Justice Clark set forth the court's opinion. It is nevertheless significant in questioning the simple idea that a religious program may receive government support if it serves a public function. If the Brennan position were adopted, it would mean that, although some or all church schools meet the secular educational standards of government, they cannot constitutionally be financially supported by government on the grounds that they serve a public or secular function. More than a public or secular purpose ought therefore to be involved. Public authorities, in carrying out a proper function of government, should do so by nonreligious means, where possible, and in other cases by means that have the least effect on religion.

Justice Felix Frankfurter, in another concurring opinion, stated this in somewhat different form in *McGowan vs. Maryland:*

> *If the value to society of achieving the object of a particular regulation is demonstrably outweighed by the impediment to which the regulation subjects those whose religious practices are curtailed by it, or if the object sought by the regulation could with equal effect be achieved by alternative means which do not substantially impede those religious practices, the regulation cannot be sustained.*[17]

The political philosophy that underlies the First Amendment is apparently set forth in the two ideas of neutrality and separation. That philosophy, in effect, asserts that government can best be protected from political division based on religion by staying out of the emotionally charged area of religious controversy. It also asserts that religious groups can most effectively be protected from government hostility by restricting the power of government to act on religious matters.[18]

Another important aspect of the neutrality-separation philosophy is the protection of nonreligious citizens and those of minority religious groups from a government allied with major religious faiths. In the ecumenical age, when Protestant–Roman Catholic rivalries may disappear, the court may increasingly have to protect non-Christians and atheists from the political power of Christians. Such a position was also set forth in *Torcaso vs. Watkins,* which stated that neither a state nor the federal government "can constitutionally pass laws or impose requirements which aid all religions as against non-believers, and neither can aid those religions based on a belief in the existence of God as against those religions founded on different beliefs."[19]

Even prior to the present ecumenical spirit, there were attacks on the political philosophy implied in "neutrality" and "separation." These attacks had as their purpose the scuttling of the idea of separation in order to make possible an "accommodation theory" or cooperative philosophy under which government could, when desirable, support religion or aid religious institutions. One difficulty with this theory is the assumption that government can act objectively and impartially to determine what is in the public interest, whereas the impulse for such action inevitably comes from pressure groups acting in their own interest.

The fact that the United States does not have and never has had an absolute separation of Church and State is sometimes used as a rationale for throwing overboard the whole idea. Robert Hutchins and a number of others who favor government aid to parochial schools argue that since there never has been an absolute separation the term is meaningless.

"The wall," said Hutchins, "has done what walls usually do: it has obscured the view. It has lent a simplistic air to the discussion of a very complicated matter. Hence it has caused confusion whenever it has been invoked. . . . The wall has been offered as a reason. It is not a reason; it is a figure of speech."[20]

Such criticism could be made of any written constitutional provisions. There never has been absolute free speech or freedom of the press in the United States. Sedition and libel laws have been adopted in spite of the Bill of Rights. The Eighth Amendment, to cite another example, provides that "cruel and unusual punishment" shall not be inflicted; yet American prisons have confined persons to solitary dungeons without clothing and with small rations of bread and water. The First Amendment and other provisions of the Bill of Rights do have an element of the absolute in them. But in another sense they are not absolute for they do require interpretation.

When anyone suggests that a constitutional provision lends "a simplistic air to the discussion of a very complicated matter," he is simply arguing against any norms or guidelines by which complicated matters can be judged. This, of course, is another way of stating the case against laws as such. No law, however simple or complex its language, can meet every human situation. It is a truism that every rule has its exceptions. So those who argue against separation of Church and State on the ground that it is "simplistic" or that there has never been an absolute separation are really arguing against any attempt to state in constitutional or legal form a guiding principle or norm.

The argument that "wall of separation" is a figure of speech, a metaphor, is convincing only to those for whom symbols are not expressive of ideas. Actually, the metaphor is *too* expressive and *too* symbolic for those who want something that is forbidden by the concept of separation of Church and State. The real problem with that section of the First Amendment which states that "Congress shall make no law respecting an establishment of religion . . ." is that it frustrates those who want Congress to aid some religious interest or institution.

In response to those who claimed that "the wall" has caused confusion, Harold Fey, at the time editor of the *Christian Century*, stated:

> the term "wall" as Jefferson used it means a distinction, a limitation, a definition of fields of competence and authority. . . . It clarifies rather than confuses thought. . . . It is a line between two orders of experience, between absolutes on one side and relativities on the other, between the deep issues of faith and the practical issues of politics. It separates two realms of authority, each of which functions best when the two are distinguished. Finally it bounds two systems of economics: the compulsory economy of a commonwealth and the voluntary economy of philanthropy.[21]

There is value then in the idea of a wall of separation even though that wall has been breached in one or more court decisions.

There are, of course, other values and other implications of the concepts of neutrality and separation. Our purpose here is simply to suggest a constitutional context in which Church–State policy as it relates to education may be discussed. In line with this, Appendix A lists the major Supreme Court cases affecting Church–State and education, together with a brief comment. The table is not intended to be exhaustive but rather to indicate something of the pattern that has developed.

2

The Changing
Protestant Context

Since World War II, Protestant thinking about Church–State relations has been undergoing significant change. A reappraisal of the role of the Protestant Church in American life has occasioned and sharpened much of the current Church–State controversy.

For centuries Protestantism as a whole, and each of the various Protestant churches, was a distinct minority in contrast to the worldwide Roman Catholic Church. American Protestants, conscious that the numerical superiority of Catholics enabled the European Church to seek and use power in Europe, dreaded both the possibility of Roman Catholic expansion in the New World and the potential drive of the Church to become dominant in American political life. Roman Catholics in America, on the other hand, have been themselves a minority within a general Protestant culture, fearing exposure of their children to Protestant ideas in the public school and experiencing various degrees of religious intolerance from the society as a whole. Contemporary Protestants, acutely aware that the centuries-old establishment of the Roman Catholic Church in Spain, Italy and Latin America had denied religious liberty to Protestants in those countries, tend to forget that after the Protestant Reformation, Lutheran, Anglican and Reformed churches became established in Germany, England, Holland, Scotland and the Scandinavian countries and that Catholics had suffered under the intolerance of a Protestant establishment.

In the United States, Protestants have been generally unaware that a general Protestant culture pervades the society as a whole, manifesting itself in the public schools in such practices as prayer and Bible reading and high school baccalaureate services conducted by Protestant ministers. So strong has been the ethos of Protestantism as to deny, until 1960, the election of a Roman Catholic to the Presidency of the United States. Protestant cultural dominance has been the topic of countless studies of American society with the pejorative label "White Anglo–Saxon Protestant" being frequently pressed into service to describe the dominating cultural ethos in the United States. The buzzing, if not the sting of the WASP must be appreciated in any attempt to understand the changing positions of the Protestant Church on the questions of religious liberty that engage contemporary America.

Such descriptions, however useful, do not necessarily increase understanding, and accuracy forces the assertion that the culture has not been Protestant in any meaningful or exact sense of that term. Rather, it has tended to reject Catholicism in the interest of a vague religious expression that is inoffensive to most Protestants, a form of cultural religion, the general outlines of which are utilitarian rather than adequately expressive of distinctive Protestant understandings. Its espousal is most frequently associated with a whole set of values that are usually connected with the phrase "our way of life" and enlisted in support of American nationalism, capitalism or military policy.

Illustrations abound of obeisance to cultural religion in behalf and support of the American way. Two will suffice to illustrate the point. In proposing that the phrase "under God" be inserted in the pledge of allegiance to the flag, Senator Homer Ferguson (R.) of Michigan said, "We know that America cannot be defended by guns, planes and ships alone. Appropriations and expenditures for defense will be of value only if the God under whom we live believes that we are in the right." Seeking to reinforce his point he continued in the same statement, "We now live in a world divided by two ideologies, one of which affirms its belief in God while the other does not."[1] Perhaps even more telling are the now famous assertions of President Eisenhower, who said, "Our government makes no sense unless it is founded in a deeply felt religious faith—and I don't care what it is." Again, "I am the most intensely religious man I know. That doesn't mean that I adhere to any sect. A democracy cannot exist without a religious base. I believe in democracy."[2]

Devotees of American cultural religion are not basically committed to a particular religious faith. In fact they shun any expression of religion that would be critical or hostile to the values embodied in their "way of life." They are content with any public ritual that links God with American values and subscribe to a vague lowest-common-denominator expression of the three major faiths of the United States. In a religious census, however, they would tend to list themselves as Protestant only to signify that they are not Jewish or Roman Catholic. While accepting a residuum of the three major religious expressions, their allegiance is not to Protestant faith but to a cultural Protestantism in which they and their fathers were reared.

This, of course, is not a uniquely American phenomenon. Millions of nominal Lutherans in Northern Europe and Roman Catholics in Southern Europe and Latin America prefer a Lutheran or a Roman Catholic culture without reference to the depths of the faith. In the United States the pervasive cultural Protestantism, frequently allied with the interests of those who would welcome some form of nondenominational Protestant religion, is totally abhorrent to church leaders and theologians. Its expressions, often non-Christian, although usually not anti-Christian or anti-Protestant in content, have led some religious interpreters to speak of an American "Protestant establishment." It has tended to oppose Roman Catholic efforts to gain government aid for parochial schools and upon occasion has demonstrated a marked hostility to Roman Catholicism even where no Catholic political effort was being made. It has been a powerful factor operating against genuine separation of Church and State. Regrettably, the fact that Protestant denominations and interchurch agencies also opposed any special status for the Roman Catholic Church often led to the falacious assumption that these bodies were cooperating in a Protestant establishment even though neither the individual denominations nor the various denominational bodies sought special status for themselves or their schools.

Two highly significant events within the present decade have, however, marked the demise of cultural Protestantism in the United States. Ended symbolically by the decision of the voters in 1960 to elect a Roman Catholic as President, much of its remaining power was denied by the decision of the Supreme Court which, in 1963, outlawed devotional exercises in the public schools. Bearing on both events is the growth of a genuinely pluralistic society. While there are still substantial Protestant majorities in most states of the Union, the large number of agnostics and humanists and the increase of the Roman Catholic and Jewish populations have enabled a more politically powerful pluralism to challenge and contain the dominant Protestant ethos.

In the face of these events it might be argued that Protestant leaders have lost their ability to mobilize their people, but there is, in fact, no evidence that the leaders of any major Protestant denomination have tried to foster or maintain a Protestant ascendancy. It is significant, rather, that the leaders of all major Protestant denominations, including Southern Baptist, refused to oppose the election of a Roman Catholic to the Presidency and openly supported the Supreme Court prayer decisions. Some Protestants would argue that the issue was never the religious membership of Roman Catholic candidates for public office so much as it was the assumption that they supported the hierarchy's effort to get public funds for church enterprises. In any event, John F. Kennedy's public commitment to separation of Church and State won the support or acquiescence of many Protestants who otherwise would openly have opposed him. The evidence now seems to indicate that membership in the Roman Catholic Church was a liability, that membership in some Protestant church is not a necessity but that a commitment to an American cultural religion is a prerequisite for candidacy for the office of President.

The decline of Protestant cultural religion was equally marked by the issues surrounding the debate on the New York Regents' prayer. During the period of reaction to the Supreme Court decision prohibiting devotional exercises in public schools, a constitutional amendment permitting such exercises was introduced in Congress by Representative Frank Becker, a Republican and Roman Catholic from New York. Enjoying the support of Cardinal Spellman and many Roman Catholics, Becker was supported also by Protestants in the South and Midwest who followed the leadership of flamboyant radio preachers, extreme-right-wing spokesmen and some of the more conservative Protestant sects.[3] Utilizing the formula "Almighty God, we acknowledge our dependence upon Thee, and we beg Thy blessing upon us, our parents, our teachers, and our country," the New York Regents' prayer was obviously nonsectarian and non-Christian and, far from being either Protestant or Catholic, a cultural religious expression that would have received wide support from Protestant denominations in the nation's earlier history. However, despite thousands of communications approving the proposed amendment and the paucity of congressmen prepared publicly to oppose it, the testimony of the National Council of Churches and of leaders of major Protestant denominations decisively killed the amendment before it could pass the Judiciary Committee. This was the more remarkable as the amendment had extensive backing in the House and influential support within the committee.

In its testimony, the General Board of the National Council of Churches asserted that "neither true religion nor good education is dependent upon the devotional use of the Bible in the public school program." The Baptist Joint Committee on Public Affairs, which includes the Southern Baptists, the largest denomination not in the National Council of Churches, reaffirmed its "conviction that laws and regulations prescribing prayers or devotional exercises do not contribute to a free exercise of religion and should not be encouraged."

The conviction of Protestant leaders that the disestablishment of cultural religion is necessary if religious liberties are to be preserved was in part an outgrowth of careful studies of Church–State issues which had been undertaken by various denominations. In May, 1963, a month prior to the Supreme Court decision, the Presbyterian General Assembly recommended to all of its churches a group of guidelines that included the following: that

> *religious observances never be held in a public school or introduced into the public school as part of its program. Bible reading in connection with courses in the American heritage, world history, literature, the social sciences and other academic subjects is completely appropriate to public school instruction. Bible reading and prayers as devotional acts tend toward indoctrination or meaningless ritual and should be omitted for both reasons.*[4]

The Lutheran Church in America and the Methodist Church also had study commissions at work well before the Supreme Court decision. The Lutheran statement, published in 1963, shortly after the prayer and Bible-reading decisions, said: "The Court has clearly made an important contribution to the cause of religious freedom."[5] The Methodist study commission took a similar position.

While the American Church–State problem has centered, in recent years, on the challenges posed by cultural religion, the early decades of the twentieth century found Protestants aggressively assertive in legislative concerns. During World War I and its aftermath, some Protestant denominations were successful in having their concept of total abstinence from alcohol translated into the Volstead Act and soon thereafter into the Eighteenth Amendment to the Constitution. When the Prohibition amendment was repealed, the churches did not support repeal. Rather, in some cases, they turned their attention to local option or to statewide efforts to preserve as much of a "dry" political area as possible.

Contemporary Protestant action in the political arena is, however, not designed to impose a Protestant ethic upon the state or to achieve government aid for Protestant projects. Most of the major denominations have come to accept a new approach to social action in harmony with the whole concept of religious liberty. For example, the Methodist Division of Temperance and Public Morals, which was a spearhead in the drive for Prohibition, has abandoned political action as a method for achieving abstinence, concentrating instead on research, education and the commitment of individual Methodists. Similarly, the National Council of Churches noted in its pronouncement "The Churches and Alcohol" that "it is more effective to win understanding than to coerce people."

Nevertheless, many denominations have social action staffs that encourage churchwide political action. Their approach is now designed to create public opinion rather than to impose church doctrine on society through regulations or law. The emphasis is on the creation of consensus through written and acted word, recognizing that consensus alone can enable the "consent of the governed" to permit legislation to endure. Specifically, this means that no church may legislate upon the rest of society its social doctrine concerning alcohol or birth control or gambling or tax support of church institutions unless that legislation has won public acceptance on a wide basis. If a local, state or national government adopts legislation against the use of alcohol or against gambling, it must be because the general population is convinced these are harmful to the public health or welfare and not because a denomination is convinced that such conduct is unbecoming a Christian. The case for or against any piece of legislation must be made in secular terms quite apart from the vested doctrinal or organizational interests of a denomination or church.

Protestant social action movements have been driven to this position by their own commitment to the concept of religious liberty. They have learned that the denial of religious liberty has generally been caused by an authoritarian or established church collaborating with government to establish rules without regard either to public opinion or to minority religious views. They insist that all moral or religious matters that concern government must stand the test of public scrutiny and win assent on the basis of their own consistency with the public welfare.

Despite the evidence cited, the movement toward genuine religious liberty is, among Protestants, far from complete. Although the movement is supported by leaders of the major Protestant denominations, thousands of laymen who give lip service to separation of Church and State do not really want to abandon the kind of general Protestant culture in which they grew up.

They are far from certain that separation should apply to their Protestant practices. For many, separation is simply a necessary principle to prevent a more aggressive church than their own from dominating the state. Further, most are unprepared to accept the new ethical dimensions required by church involvement in the problems of society. Many of these have remained loyal to their local churches but have become critical of the National Council of Churches, their denominational leaders and especially church boards and publications that represent or portray active involvement in the social struggle.

Furthermore, many fear the completion of the process of cultural religious disestablishment out of the threat that genuine religious liberty may create a power vacuum into which either Roman Catholic religious forms or some form of humanism will flow, resulting in the dominance of American culture by a non-Protestant ethos.

More pragmatically, many are unprepared to accept the new challenges required by church involvement in society when accompanied by total separation from the state. In almost every Protestant denomination there are church-related institutions such as hospitals, colleges and homes for the elderly, which, though clearly owned and administered by the church, are not reluctant to accept governmental funding or tacit support. Presidents and administrators of such institutions, highly influential in their denominations, are not at all averse to receiving government loans and grants and often comprise a built-in lobby for government aid to such church-related enterprises. In the section considering state aid to church-related institutions at the National Council of Churches Study Conference on Church and State held in February, 1964, in Columbus, Ohio, the administrators made it impossible to vote on a motion that "colleges qualifying for state aid must refrain from discrimination on the basis of race, creed, or national origin in the selection of students and faculty and in any religious requirements in matters of discipline." Yet an informal poll revealed ten favoring and fourteen opposing government grants to colleges with active relations to a church. Sixteen favored and eight opposed government loans to such colleges.

The administrators of Protestant church-related institutions are not proponents of special aid to Protestant agencies, but many do not want to see so complete a separation of Church and State as to foreclose government aid to religious institutions. The fact that certain Protestant-related institutions do receive government funds tends to make some Protestants feel guilty either about opposing any government aid to any church institution or about imposing secular criteria for the making of such grants. The result is that these vested Protestant interests tend to encourage a mood that is not averse to an establishment of religion in general. By and large it is liberal churchmen who think in terms of such church cooperation with government and tend to believe that the United States is so mature a democracy as not to use any advantage of government financial aid to control or influence the churches. Their concept is that the church should be the willing partner or agent of government in activities of service to those in need of public health, welfare and education, partly because the problems of modern society are so great that the churches cannot deal adequately with them through their own resources.

Theological influences from without have added yeast to the ferment of Protestant reappraisals of the Church and State controversy, most notable of which has been the impact of the Roman Catholic ecumenical movement. Unquestionably some Protestants have favored separation of Church and State because it has been the only way to deny aid to Roman Catholic enterprises. Those so motivated rarely if ever questioned any manifestation of Protestant privilege and failed to appreciate that when dependent on an anti-Catholic bias, support of the concept of separation of Church and State will evaporate if the bias disappears. This happened to some ministers and laymen in Missouri. One prominent clergyman in metropolitan Kansas City who, in 1963, had opposed the use of public funds for bus transportation to parochial schools changed his mind as the result of extensive contacts and dialogue with Roman Catholic priests. Admitting that all the arguments against it were still valid, he now had no enthusiasm for opposing a Roman Catholic campaign for free public transportation to parochial schools.

A denominational leader who has never shown any anti-Catholic bias nevertheless protested the decision in 1965 of the Missouri

Council of Churches to oppose public bus service to parochial schools but did not protest it in 1963. He was concerned lest opposition to a measure involving Roman Catholics might damage the growing ecumenical relations. Another denominational leader was vigorously opposed to the parochial school bus bill but felt it should be fought by a group organized specifically for this purpose so that the Council of Churches would not appear to be spearheading the opposition. Such attitudes may be seen as signs of ecumenical immaturity reminiscent of those unemancipated whites who cannot publicly oppose an idea or program sponsored by Negroes for fear of being thought prejudiced or hostile to the civil rights movement. Certainly, the ecumenical dialogue, if it is genuine, must be able to stand the strain of political as well as religious difference.

The affirmative aspect of the dialogue between Catholics and Protestants was clearly evidenced in the presence of Roman Catholic and Jewish observers at the National Council of Churches 1964 Study Conference on Church and State. These observers were invited to present their positions in section meetings and their views were given consideration along with those of other denominations. The result was a principled discussion of Church–State matters free from bias against any particular group. In such meetings, the Jews have made significant contributions, having sensitized Christians to the injustice that minorities suffer at the hands of an establishment of religion, however vague and general it may be.

Within the Protestant Church, the movement for church renewal is also having a significant effect on the shape of contemporary Protestant thinking. Concerning itself less with institutional empires such as church hospitals or educational systems and committed instead to meeting human need, the movement forcefully reminds Protestants that millions of human beings are left unsatisfied when government aid to church colleges chiefly serves middle- and upper-class students or subsidizes church-sponsored homes for senior citizens of the same general economic position.

The critique offered by the church renewal movement points up the primary problem of Protestants with respect to religious liberty, that being the acceptance of government funds for community welfare projects and for higher education. While Protestants, as a rule, give very little thought to asking government aid to finance any form of religious or doctrinal education, their willing acceptance of government funds for church work or the use of the church for government work raises profound questions, not simply of religious liberty, but of the mission of the church as well. The church has a unique mission to take the gospel to all men and to witness to the redemptive love of God manifest in Jesus Christ. That witness is compromised if it is made by a subsidized agent of government. As Dean Kelley of the Department of Social Justice of the National Council of Churches has so aptly noted, institutions "are shaped by the sources of their support and cannot readily leave some and go hunting new ones without jeopardizing the vast flow of resources which is the lifeblood of the institution."

The church will find that in collaborating with government its critique of the conditions of poverty and injustice found within the social and political structures of the established order will be severely compromised. While liberal churchmen may place their hope in governmental appropriations for the solution of social problems, they frequently fail to understand that government action for social amelioration seeks primarily to prevent disruption of the social order rather than to deal fundamentally with the structural problems at their root. Being misled by its own good intentions and available government resources, the church runs the danger of becoming a channel for government projects and thereby invariably departs from its own unique mission. The church is the church only when it is true to its own witness, unfettered by ties to the interests of any economic class, race or political group. When related to any partisan interests, its universality is compromised and its witness is vitiated.

The church's mission is to all men, regardless of culture or nationality. When, through cooperation with any government, it becomes so identified with a specific social order and power structure the church runs the deep danger of incurring the resentment of those opposed to or oppressed by the government. In our time we know, to our sorrow, the implications such alliances have for the church's overseas witness. Evidence abounds of the tendency in underdeveloped and Communist worlds to identify the church as an agent or collaborator of the Western powers, specifically America, and objective evidence of government use of the church to carry out government programs further diminishes the church's credibility in countries outside the West.

In conclusion, six reasons may be identified for Protestants and all churchmen to favor government neutrality with respect to religion:

1. Neutrality prevents the government from determining church policy, whether directly or indirectly.
2. Neutrality disallows the church to seek special privileges from government which are denied to nonreligious citizens or minority religious groups.
3. The church is healthier and stronger if it assumes responsibility both for financing its own resources and for stimulating its members to accept full responsibility for its programs.
4. By operating independently of government aid, the church denies the government the opportunity to impose compulsory tithes on all taxpayers, believers and nonbelievers alike.
5. By refusing financial support or special privilege, the church is free to engage in prophetic criticism of the government and to work for social justice.
6. The church's witness in other cultures is greater if it is not identified with Western culture or with one or more specific governments.

To summarize the findings of this chapter: Protestant thinking has been affected by its own concern for religious liberty, by the ecumenical dialogue, by the involvement of church social action movements in the larger secular community and by the concern of both radical and conservative churchmen. The resistance to change by some conservative churchmen together with the vested interest of church-related colleges, hospitals and other welfare projects and a philosophy of cooperation with any welfare state goal, has to some degree thwarted the drive for the separation of Church and State. All of these forces are involved in the changing context within the Protestant churches which create the climate for the current discussion of Church, State and education.

3

The New
Roman Catholic Context

Roman Catholic doctrine and practice with respect to religious liberty has undergone significant change within the past two decades and, most notably so, as a consequence of the deliberations of the second Vatican Council (1962–63). As is the case with changes in Protestant thought, the new directions taken by the Catholics have caused controversy both on the American scene and within the Church.

The traditional Roman Catholic position that is used to justify efforts at establishing that religion was described in the volume *Catholic Principles of Politics* (1960 edition), written by the Reverend John A. Ryan, formerly director of the Department of Social Action of the National Catholic Welfare Conference, and the Reverend Francis J. Boland, head of the department of politics at the University of Notre Dame. Their book, carrying the imprimatur of Cardinal Spellman, quotes Pope Leo XIII (1878–1903) as declaring:

the State must not only "have care for religion," but recognize the true *religion professed by the Catholic Church. It is a thoroughly logical position. If the State is under moral compulsion to profess and promote religion, it is obviously obliged to profess and promote only the religion that is true; for no individual, no group of individuals, no society, no State is justified in supporting error or in according to error the same recognition as to truth.*[1]

Fathers Ryan and Boland write that in practice, recognition of Roman Catholicism by the state as the only true religion could "have full application only to the completely Catholic State. This means a political community that is either exclusively, or almost exclusively, made up of Catholics." Where full application is not possible the Church has authority to use such direct or indirect power as is feasible "to affect political affairs having a religious or moral aspect."[2]

A more liberal group in the Roman Catholic Church, whose chief American spokesman was the late Reverend John Courtney Murray, S.J., professor of theology at Woodstock College, challenged this point of view in part while giving it endorsement in part. Father Murray held that the Roman Catholic Church is the one true church but believed that this does not require state defense or promotion of it. In discussing the question whether "heretical propaganda does spiritual harm" he wrote:

Granted: nevertheless this is not the kind of harm that secular government as the agent of public order, is bound by its office to ward off from its citizens. The protection of her members in the possession of their faith is the task of the Church; *it is a spiritual, not a political task. And if the Church is too weak to perform this task successfully, she does not by that fact acquire a juridical right to invoke the coercive strength of secular government. . . . If it be asserted that the temporal power is distinct from the spiritual power, sovereign in a limited order, distinct from the spiritual order, it cannot be that the distinctions should suddenly vanish to permit the temporal order to become attached to the Church as her "secular arm" to minister to needs that are not secular but spiritual.*[3]

Father Murray rejected the idea of a legal establishment of the Roman Catholic Church, accepted the fact of religious pluralism in the United States and insisted that the political society or state should be secular in its operation. He nevertheless recognized the right of the Church to influence and permeate society through the convictions and consciences of Roman Catholics as citizens.

> *The Christian then as citizen, in the full panoply of his democratic rights, prolongs, as it were, this action of the church into the temporal order, in all the matters in which Christian doctrine and law has [sic] implications for the life and law and government of society.*[4]

Nor is Murray alone in challenging the view of the traditionalists. The Vatican Council itself revealed the differences of opinion within the Roman Catholic Church on relationships between Church and State. In general there were three approaches taken in the discussions. The first approach was that of full religious liberty for everyone. Those who held this position recognized that in the new conditions of religious pluralism in the West and Communist hostility or "neutrality" in the East, the Roman Catholic Church could not expect a special status or special privileges from the State. The Archbishop of Prague, Cardinal Beran, referred to pre-Communist government support of the Roman Catholic Church, which aided his church at the expense of Protestants:

> *By such acts, the secular arm, wishing or pretending to serve the Catholic Church, in reality left a hidden wound in the hearts of the people. This trauma was an obstacle to religious progress and offered, and still offers facile material for agitation to the enemies of the church.*[5]

A second group, chiefly conservative Italian and Spanish bishops, argued for preservation of the special status enjoyed by the Roman Catholic Church, including concordats between the Vatican and other governments. A third point of view, prevailing in the final document, The Declaration of Religious Liberty, affirmed the right of each individual to freedom of conscience and recognized the right of individuals and organized groups to practice and propagate their beliefs so long as they do not interfere with the "public order."

The final document of The Declaration of Religious Liberty, widely hailed by both Protestant churchmen and many in secular life, falls far short of the religious liberty guaranteed in the United States Constitution. The Jesuit weekly *America* acknowledged this on October 2, 1965, in its editorial on the declaration, saying, "It is perhaps necessary to remind Americans that the Council is not about to enact the First Amendment of the United States Constitution as a Catholic Doctrine."

The Declaration of Religious Liberty falls short of the First Amendment and of most non-Catholic concepts of liberty at a number of points. It affirms, for example, "traditional Catholic doctrine on the moral duty of men and societies toward the true religion and toward the one Church of Christ." The declaration is specific that "this one true religion subsists in the [Roman] Catholic and Apostolic Church. . . ." It also indicates that the declaration does not, in given circumstances, prevent a particular religious group from receiving "special civil recognition" from the state provided that "the right of all citizens and religious bodies to freedom in religious matters be recognized and protected." Conditional clauses in the declaration further tend to qualify genuine liberty. Such clauses as "within due limits" or "provided that just public order be observed," or "a proper guardianship of public morality" provide loopholes for national hierarchies and governments. In the January–February, 1966, *Liberty*, W. L. Emerson points out:

> *That these provisos leave dangerously open to interpretation the circumstances in which the state may interfere with the liberty of subjects was underlined on the council floor itself when Cardinal Enrico Dante said that the argument that "religious liberty can be restricted for considerations based on the common good and public order leaves the question at the mercy of various conceptions of the common good and public order!"*

Many non-Catholic spokesmen, in hailing an advance in Roman Catholic doctrine, have tended to overlook yet another point where the declaration falls short of genuine religious liberty. For, while its advance was the repudiation of the traditional position that "error has no rights" and the affirmation that persons rather than beliefs have rights, the document falls short in its dualism. It perpetuates the claim that religious liberty for the Roman Catholic Church is grounded in divine law and the special status given to her as the one true church, whereas for non-Catholics the basis for liberty is limited to belief in human dignity or "civil right." Asserting that "the freedom of the Church is the fundamental principle in what concerns the relations between the Church and governments and the whole civil order," the declaration claims this as "a sacred freedom" which "is so much the property of the Church that to act against it is to act against the will of God." Such rights, in turn, are intended to provide the Roman Catholic Church "the independence which is necessary for the fulfillment of her divine mission. This independence is precisely what the authorities of the Church claim in society."

In contrast to the divine authority of the Roman Catholic Church, other religious groups and all men "possess the civil right" of religious liberty. Significantly, this civil right is not set forth in the absolute terms reserved for the Roman Catholic Church but is due to present day circumstances. "The fact is that *men of the present day* want to be able freely to profess their religion in private and public; indeed, religious freedom has already been declared to be a civil right in most constitutions . . ." [emphasis added]. Again, the declaration states: "The Council exhorts Catholics, and it directs a plea to all men, most carefully to consider how greatly necessary religious freedom is especially *in the present condition* of the human family" [emphasis added].

It is notable that the declaration concentrates on the obligation of the government and of society to safeguard religious liberty but nowhere does it speak of religious liberty within the church. The net result is that the influence of the church, insofar as it continues authoritarian traditions and discipline, is against religious liberty. A good illustration is found in the impact of Roman Catholic authoritarianism upon students and pupils in their educational institutions, which problem a Roman Catholic theologian discussed in these words:

> *Since the great majority of Catholic institutions of higher learning developed under the care of religious communities, orders like the Jesuits, Dominicans, etc., the same problems that beset the religious life filtered down to the administration of the school. When all religious communities were run under an officially paternalistic regime, it was natural that academic administrators should adopt the same attitudes toward students under their care that their own religious superiors were adopting toward them.*[6]

Those who criticize the Roman Catholic Church's new position on religious liberty generally make the point that it is difficult, if not impossible, for a church that denies liberty to its own laymen, priests and bishops to do much for liberty for others outside the Church. The Reverend Christopher C. Webber, an Episcopalian, has said that Catholic structural reform must begin with a system "in which no layman yet has a voice, no parish priest, bishop or cardinal is elected, in which no representative forms exist." He added in discussing such questions as attendance at other religious ceremonies or participation in weddings between non-Romans: "the basic theory is still that you must be guided in all such things by the hierarchy; that they will decide what is best for you and what you may do." Father Webber concludes by saying: "When all rules and power are placed in the hands of one man, however able and liberal and well advised, error is almost certain."[7]

Apart from its assertions, The Declaration of Religious Liberty must be viewed in terms of its context and general spiritual impact. The context is most important, as the declaration, adopted by the Vatican Council, is only one statement among many that was promulgated by Pope Paul VI. The Council's new attitude toward Protestants, Jews and even atheists is not one of hostility but one of understanding and dialogue. That the rights of others will be respected is more likely in such an atmosphere than in a climate of hatred or rivalry or hostility. The ecumenical spirit that is manifested goes beyond mere personal gestures or polite listening to the views of others. Protestant biblical and theological scholarship, for example, is taken seriously and examined with respect. Indeed, Roman Catholic publications give increasing attention to developments in the Protestant world, not just for purposes of critical analysis, but for purposes of information and appreciation. The Jesuit weekly *America*, for example, stated editorially on October 9, 1965:

> *Protestants whose devotion to religious toleration has not always been as deep as the Whig theory of history would have them believe, may none the less take credit for the attitude of the bishops from traditionally Protestant lands. It was not fear of Protestant persecution, but the experience of freedom that led these bishops to support the declaration on religious liberty so earnestly.*

Certainly the major impact of the Vatican Council decrees in general and The Declaration of Religious Liberty in particular, lies in the over-all interpretation given them by the Church itself. If the hierarchy emphasizes the positive achievements, renewal of the Church and respect for others of different religious persuasion will continue. If it emphasizes the conditional clauses and minimizes the underlying spirit of the deliberations, a wholly different image of the Church will result. Indeed, in many countries the effect of the Vatican Council has been profoundly creative and innovative. John Cogley, a Roman Catholic layman speaking at the National Catholic Education Association's 1966 convention said that Catholicism is "undergoing a revolutionary change" and, he indicated, has had a revolutionary impact. "Some of the Vatican Council Fathers," he said, "apparently thought that we would have ourselves a nice quiet revolution. . . . But that simply is not how revolution works."

The new hope for religious liberty arises not entirely from the positive statements in the declaration but from the fact that they open the door to other changes. The direction of changes already made may suggest others that should and can take place. Since the declaration is primarily a pragmatic and juridical document, the expectations springing from it and the reaction to it can expand its usefulness for all those who believe in liberty. It, as well as other Vatican Council decrees, have tended to eliminate the fear of many Protestants and others in America that the goal of the Roman Catholic Church in the United States is political domination of the nation. The reason, of course, is that the Council acknowledged the facts of modern religious pluralism as well as the need to respect other religious groups.

Yet it would be a superficial analysis if one assumed that the Church–State problem in the United States had been solved by the new accent on ecumenism or religious liberty. Americans have always associated genuine religious liberty with more than the right to free exercise of one's faith, referring to the First Amendment, which included two ideas, one guaranteeing the "free exercise" of religion and the other prohibiting laws "respecting an establishment of religion." From a Roman Catholic point of view, the Church–State problem arises from the conflict between the free exercise clause and the establishment clause. This conflict is no more clearly evident than in the area of education, for The Declaration of Religious Liberty speaks of the right of parents "to determine . . . the kind of religious education that their children are to receive." This means that government "must acknowledge the right of parents to make a genuinely free choice of schools. . . ."

According to the Council's Declaration on Christian Education, free choice has nothing to do with parental options to send a child to a nonchurch school, for "the Council also reminds Catholic parents of the duty of entrusting their children to Catholic schools." Rather, free choice means "that public subsidies are paid out in such a way that parents are truly free to choose" a church school that either charges tuition or would otherwise have to be supported by the Church. The decree also asserts that the Roman Catholic "family which has the primary duty of imparting education needs the help of the whole community." This is further defined as a civic duty "to give them aid—and moreover, as the common good demands, to build schools and institutions." The decree goes on to say that "in a special way the duty of educating belongs to the Church—especially because she has the responsibility of announcing the way of salvation to all men. . . ."

In this way the Vatican Council has woven the idea of government aid to church schools into its position on religious liberty.

Such a broadening of the idea of liberty to include state subsidy of any institution a person wants to patronize would logically involve not only state subsidy of church schools but of churches, and entails subsidies of other educationally supportive institutions of the Roman Church.

The establishment clause in the First Amendment was designed to prevent just such an absolutist concept that religious liberty or free exercise demands public subsidy. Holding that such a concept of religious liberty surely violates the liberties of others, Thomas Jefferson, in the preamble to the Bill for the Establishing of Religious Freedom in Virginia, wrote:

> ". . . to compel a man to furnish contributions of money for the propagation of opinions which he disbelieves and abhors, is sinful and tyrannical; even the forcing him to support this or that teacher of his own religious persuasion, is depriving him of the comfortable liberty of giving his contributions to the particular pastor whose morals he would make his pattern. . . ."

The mark of an establishment of religion is not limited to domination of public officials by a religious group or groups or the acknowledgment by government of the legal supremacy of a particular church. It is also evident in the use of law and taxation to coerce people to support a religious program or institution that they are not inwardly convinced they should support, or to coerce them to support it in a particular way or with a different amount of money than they would voluntarily give. The establishment clause is therefore essential to religious liberty and for this reason the First Amendment joins the free exercise clause with the no-establishment clause to provide genuine religious liberty for everyone.

It is at this point that the cardinal weakness of the Vatican Council's Declaration of Religious Liberty is found. It does not reject the idea of an establishment of religion but actually lays the groundwork for special status for the Roman Catholic Church. The provision that other groups and persons shall have religious freedom does not extend to freedom for nonbelievers from taxation for church schools.

The question of community subsidy of church schools is so crucial to religious liberty because of the key role the schools play in shaping the life of the nation. There is a fundamental contradiction between the idea of no establishment of religion and the idea that "in a special way the duty of the state is to subsidize such church schools."

It would be a mistake, however, either to minimize the danger to religious liberty of the various efforts to win government subsidy for church schools or to assume that all Roman Catholics are committed to securing such subsidies. It would be an even greater mistake to assume that a commitment on the part of some Roman Catholics to secure such subsidy for educational purposes predisposes them to oppose religious liberty at other points. A case in point is the traditional Catholic ban on birth control. In New York State the Catholic Welfare Committee strongly opposed the repeal of a law prohibiting the sale or distribution of birth control devices, while in Massachusetts, Cardinal Cushing, in facing a similar situation, was quoted as saying it did not seem reasonable to him "to forbid in civil law a practice that can be considered a matter of private morality."[8] At a later date, he went a step further, saying: "I do not see where I have the obligation to impose my will on those who do not accept the faith I do."[9]

Nevertheless the weight of Roman Catholic thinking on elementary and secondary education seems more concerned with "justice" or "freedom of choice" for Roman Catholics than with religious liberty for the entire community.

4

The Secular Context

The Supreme Court decisions on Bible reading and prayer dramatically emphasized the secular nature of the public school. As a result, a number of Protestants and Roman Catholics publicly expressed their fear that a religiously neutral public school was leading to the establishment of a pseudo-religion, which they called secularism. Unfortunately, those who take this position are generally not very precise about what secularism means. To some it is simply the absence of formal religious expression in the public schools. To others it may be humanism or naturalism or atheism or the enthronement of science.

For clarity of thought, it would be well to look at the Latin roots of the word "secular" and its early Christian meaning. The word itself comes from the Latin "saeculum," which means "this age" but has also been translated as "this generation" or "this world." It had a particular meaning to the early Christian church, whose leaders believed that the power of governments, as well as all other power, came from God. They understood political authority as the secular authority that God had ordained for the present age, or *saeculum*. The church, in contrast, was seen as the community of those who had already entered into the age to come. The word "secular" thus came to be applied to the present age, which the early Christians confidently expected to end with the ushering in of the Kingdom of God. When the Christian expectation of an early coming of the Kingdom did not materialize, the word "secular" gradually took on additional meaning for the church. The priests and lay brothers of the church who chose to renounce the world by living in monastic communities were differentiated from those priests who remained in the world and who were then and are now called *secular* priests. Since the structures of church discipline and life were considered sacred, those that were not ecclesiastically controlled were called secular. As a consequence, the secular state or the secular school is still negatively defined as a state or school that is not controlled directly or indirectly by any religious group or is not itself characterized by religious activity.

If a secular state or school is one without religious activity or control, there is no necessity to think of it as antireligious. The word "secular" merely implies the nonsacred, or that which is nonreligious, in nature.

The Supreme Court has properly assumed that a secular school is neither negatively nor affirmatively religious but consciously neutral in its attitude toward religion. By definition, a school or state that advocates theism or atheism or naturalism or humanism is taking a religious position. The Soviet Union is not a secular state, because it takes a negative position with respect to theism by attempting to evangelize for an atheistic center of loyalty. We too often mistakenly identify as secular a state that seeks to make itself, the party or some political and economic system the supreme value in life. Such a state is not truly secular but has sought only to deify its own political perspective and position, a position the Bible calls idolatrous.

A secular state is a political necessity in a religiously pluralist society. In the United States there are 83 separate religious bodies, each exceeding fifty thousand members, and at least an additional 200 smaller groups. There are also millions of people who belong to no church. Sixty-four per cent are church members, and 36 per cent are not.[1] It is politically necessary that such a state be neutral not only as between religious groups but also as between religious and nonreligious groups. This necessity lies in the fact that an official religious position, or government support of religion, involves discrimination against those citizens who reject religion. Similarly, an antireligious position would discriminate against those citizens who favor religion. It would be impossible to be completely impartial in dealing with 83 or 283 groups on any basis other than neutrality.

There is also a theological necessity for the secular state. Christian belief in the incarnation means that God works in and through persons, that every human being has a unique worth and is inviolable as a person. Consequently, if persons are not free to state their opposition to religion, to churches or to their doctrines, the divine criticism of human religious practices cannot be expressed. Obviously something of value is lost if any son of God is silenced.

Since God works through persons, in our theological understanding, a state that takes a position in favor of or in opposition to religion, or that establishes a specific church or religion in general, is acting against the freedom of men granted by God. Therefore, only by being consciously neutral may the state guarantee religious liberty and full respect to all persons, whether they be religious, religious nonconformists or opponents of religion. Consequently, the state and public agencies like the public schools must be secular to protect our religious assumptions about the nature of man and the inviolability of his conscience quite as much as they should be secular for political reasons.

Many Christians, both Protestant and Roman Catholic, are advocates of a secular state when they are a minority but are not so vocal in support of it when they are a majority. For example, the Archbishop of Bombay, Valerian Cardinal Gracias, lauded the secular nature of the Indian state with the following statement: "As rightly said by Prime Minister Nehru, a secular state does not mean a godless state, but one in which no particular religion is favored and all religious beliefs are given freedom to practice and propagate."[2] But neither cardinals nor bishops have asked that Spain become a secular state. Protestants point to "Catholic Spain" as an illustration of a nation determined, in large part, by the influence of the Roman Catholic hierarchy.

The Roman Catholic Church has surely suffered from the identification of Church and State in Spain, just as the Dutch Reformed Church has been seriously weakened as a result of its influence with the government of the Union of South Africa.

Christianity in general has suffered in Asia and Africa from the identification of America as a "Christian nation," particularly when people in those continents see our policies as imperialist or racist. There are therefore pragmatic as well as theological and political reasons for a secular state.

It is sometimes argued that if the rights of conscience of a non-Christian, non-Protestant or non-Catholic minority conflict with the customary religious practices of the majority, then minority rule exists. The question "Don't the majority have rights, too?" then becomes strident. But the secular state and the secular school are not intended to be the instruments of either majority or minority religious groups; rather they are intended to be neutral for the political, theological and pragmatic reasons already suggested. The constitutional principles of separation of Church and State and of neutrality give legal significance to our political and religious assumptions about the nature of man and his rights of conscience. It does not give to the minority the opportunity to dictate to the majority. It recognizes the rights of each person, whether in the majority or in a minority. Rights are limits against governmental activity, whether such government is government by majority, by committee, by temporary public opinion or by a "strong man" in a given office.

The word "secular," which we have discussed in the context of a secular state, is clearly distinct in meaning from the word "secularism." *Webster's Universal Dictionary* gives this definition of secularism:

> *Supreme or exclusive attention to the affairs of this life; specifically, an ethical system founded on natural morality, which seeks the development of the physical, moral and intellectual nature of man to the highest possible point, as the immediate duty of life, advocating practical sufficiency of natural morality apart from theism or religion, and choosing as its method of procedure the promotion of human improvement by material means.*

The *Encyclopedia Britannica* indicates that the word "secularism" refers to "the system of social ethics associated with the name of G. J. Holyoake," an Englishman who launched a periodical, *The Reasoner,* in 1846 and who wrote a book entitled *A Public Discussion on Christianity and Secularism.* The *Encyclopedia's* article says: "as the word implies, secularism is based solely on considerations of practical morality with a view to the physical, social and moral improvement of society. It neither affirms nor denies the theistic premises of religion, and is thus a particular variety of utilitarianism."

It is also possible to define secularism as a philosophy that is concerned with the immediate, rather than with ultimate, questions. It denies the relevance of religion to political, economic and other social expressions of life.

Secularism is also to be distinguished from secularization, which is a historical process by which society ceases to be dominated by the church. Secularization was evident in the popularization of education when laymen developed a body of knowledge and tools of learning so that priests and monks no longer had a monopoly on education. Secularization also occurred when scholars revolted against the narrowness, intolerance and dogmatism of the church. Instead of finding all truth in theology, men turned to philosophical and scientific investigation. The contributions of Galileo, Copernicus, Darwin and others who were attacked by the church were so significant that even religiously devoted men tended to avoid identification of their scholarship with religious ideas or institutions in order to avoid religious censorship or controversy.

In discussing secularism, it may be helpful to note that some persons think of any movement alien to or not part of the church as secularist. The real issue for them is not the rejection of religion as irrelevant to life but the rejection of ecclesiasticism. In the instance of the neutral public school, it is not simply that it is called secularist, but any lay school not under church control is similarly labeled. Quite obviously, Protestants, with their emphasis on the priesthood of all believers, would be less likely to identify a lay school with secularism than those who think of true religion in terms of one true church controlled by a hierarchy.

But both Protestants and Roman Catholics have a common tendency to point an accusing finger charging secularism to the public school or certain other nonecclesiastical movements. Evidence, however, exists that the mood of secularism is not unrelated to the life of the church. Simply because a large portion of the American population are church members does not guarantee that they are less secularist in their economic, political and social activity than non-Christians. Although there are important exceptions here and there, the churches as a whole have not generally acted as if they considered religion relevant to the problems of urban, national or international life.

On the question of human relations, the church has followed, rather than led, political and social movements for the ending of segregation or the achieving of equal employment opportunity for Negroes. The churches are lagging behind the public schools and other public agencies in desegregating. Many ministers and laymen look to the government to force the general community into unsegregated relationships with which most of the Christian community is regrettably not yet prepared to experiment. The churches have done all too little in the past twenty-five years to challenge the idea that the present economic order, by simple existence, is the American way of life and hence immune to moral criticism. In practice, churches dependent on their income from successful businessmen have tended to identify with the materialism of our culture. Wealth and power are the badges of success, and our weapons of mass destruction are its guarantors. Occasionally the Pope or Protestant leaders issue pious warnings, but no church has concentrated its efforts on any of the great moral questions such as war, population explosion, economic exploitation and civil liberties, to the degree that the Roman Catholic church has devoted its energies to seeking government aid for parochial schools or Protestant churches to prohibition.

It might be argued that the secularism in the churches is actually a by-product of what youngsters have been taught in the public schools. But this does not explain the similar attitudes of the graduates of Lutheran and Roman Catholic parochial schools, or the attitudes of many clergymen who have had extensive training in Protestant and Roman Catholic theological schools.

The Reverend John L. McKenzie, S.J., a leading Roman Catholic scholar, in an address to parochial school teachers in St. Louis, said that

". . . the Catholic school has obviously failed to communicate to many of its graduates a fair notion of what Christian love means. We have not even communicated to them that benevolent humanitarianism in virtue of which those who are not Catholics or who are agnostics support the principles of racial justice. We have sent them out into the world having memorized the catechism and scarcely anything else and trained them to a certain number of devotional exercises, and when they enter a world in which racial bigotry is the prevailing way of thought they have absolutely no way to deal with it. They accept it because it is the thinking of the community in which they live."[3]

The same observation could be made with equal force about the vast majority of Protestants.

The fact of the matter is that the churches have tended to concentrate on ultimate questions of theological significance and have paid all too little attention to the application of biblical ethics to current problems. When the clergy of the various churches do turn their attention to immediate problems they tend to speak in general terms in order to avoid the offence of specific application. Some clergymen ignore altogether the social implications of religion to concentrate exclusively on the liturgy and the teaching of personal piety. The result of these tendencies in the churches is that the application of religious convictions to business, labor, government and international affairs has been so glaring in its absence that religion has ceased to be relevant at these points even for many in the church.

Some churches contribute to the secularism of our society in other ways. The effort to get or maintain government support for religion is itself a method of encouraging secularism. The insistence by some church groups on devotional exercises in the public schools is not a contribution to genuine religion. In fact, one of the attorneys defending the use of prayer and Bible reading before the Supreme Court contended that these practices were not really religious! What he may have meant is that an otherwise religious ritual has been secularized by taking it into the public marketplace, watering it down enough to make it unobjectionable to a large segment of the community and using it before a captive audience that does not necessarily share in the deeper common faith out of which prayer and Bible reading flow.

If we examine the effort at establishment by seeking government support for church schools or other enterprises, we see that the danger of secularization is always present. In Kansas City during the summer of 1965 the Roman Catholic diocese sought and received government money for the preschool program known as Operation Headstart. One of the conditions imposed by the government in granting these funds was that there would be no religious worship or instruction. In the same city the Methodist Inner City Parish decided not to apply for public funds partly our of conviction that church agencies should be self-supporting and also because it wanted its preschool summer program to be free to include worship and religious education.

Church financing can also contribute to secularism if the funds come from government or endowment. The raising of money from laymen, on the other hand, requires some degree of involvement with their lives. This means participation in and affirmative recognition of the movement of secular thought and action that occupy so large a part of the laymen's vocational and extravocational interests. When laymen come to believe that the church is not relevant to the problems they face, they either drift away from the church or seek solutions unrelated to its position.

That so much secularism arises among church members and that the actions of the church contribute to secularism may signify to an objective observer that it is simply a case of the "pot calling the kettle black" when clergymen call the public schools secularist. The secularist similarities suggest that the churches have no right to turn their criticism on public agencies until they have done some housecleaning. This, however, is an inadequate commentary on the problem.

Some typical criticisms by religious leaders should therefore be instructive. A Religious News Service dispatch from Washington, June 17, 1963, quoted Dr. Robert A. Cooke, president of the National Association of Evangelicals, as saying that the Supreme Court ruling against Bible reading and prayer "opens the door for the full establishment of secularism as a negative form of religion." Another R.N.S. dispatch from New York, June 18, 1963, reported that "U.S. Roman Catholic Bishops and spokesmen have generally deplored the Supreme Court decision. . . . Comment from these church leaders expressed deep concern that complete secularization of American public education would result. . . ." The same dispatch reported that "several Catholic churchmen criticized the ruling on grounds that it establishes the 'religion' of secular humanism in the public school system and discriminates against parents who want a religious education for their children."

There is an assumption in all these statements that because teachers and principals are forbidden to hold devotional exercises or teach for religious commitment that the teachers themselves are nonreligious. Fortunately, the critics of the public schools never go so far as to suggest that there should be a religious test for schoolteaching. Nor do the critics cite any evidence that the nation's schoolteachers are more atheist or less active in their churches than members of any other professional or vocational group.

A further assumption may be found in these statements that the absence of a formal expression of religion is the essence of secularism. It is possible to suggest that theism may be implicit in any teacher's attitude toward his pupils and in his actual teaching without explicit teaching of religious doctrines. If God is love, as Jesus stated, and if a teacher by attitude and teaching inspires his pupils to value and apply cooperation and love in his relationships, can this be called secularism? Does the Supreme Court ruling prohibit such teaching? Not at all!

Clergymen are simply mistaken if they assume that all education and all culture must be explicitly related to theological doctrines. They must recognize that, as one God created and sustains the world, then all truth is unitary. God is truth as well as love, and the truth of science or history is not to be rejected as alien to religion because it is framed in nonreligious terminology or doctrines. The task of Christians and Jews is to relate the truths of religion to the truths learned in the schools.

As Rabbi Arthur Gilbert has put it, "Our faith compels us to be in and of the world, to work at it and with it. There is no genuine distinction between the secular and the holy. All is of God and is under God's judgment. Our task is to sanctify life by dedicating it completely, all of it, to His will."[4] In similar vein, Rabbi Gilbert adds:

> *Judaism continues to remind Christianity of its own essential doctrine that God is not known by dogmas, defined or redefined, reformed or counter-reformed, but He is revealed in history when the Word becomes event. The Jewish search for a righteous act is counter-balance to the Christian quest for a unifying creed.*[5]

Other questions need to be asked. Why should the church attack ethical teaching and conduct by public-school teachers only because they do not use a Christian or religious rationale? If children are taught ethical values in the public schools so that there is respect for personality, and human dignity replaces human abasement, can this be denigrated as secularism?

Instead of attacking the public schools as secularist, the churches should understand the purpose and function of a secular school. A truly secular school does not teach theism or alternatives to theism in an attempt to commit students to a religious position. Where such teaching is attempted, criticism by religious spokesmen ought to be specific and based on clear evidence. In any case, the blanket indictments implied in the word "secularism" make it a convenient label for something that may not exist except in the mind of the attacker.

The churches, in point of fact, should recognize the contribution of secular forces and movements. The secularist, as we suggested earlier, tends to ignore theological ultimates. In so doing, he tends to emphasize the immediate or obvious duty. Instead of being critical of this tendency, the church should welcome it as a constructive antidote to her own tendency of exclusive concentration on ultimate matters. The secular impulse to the more immediate, being more likely to eventuate in specific actions, should become a prod to the churches to talk less in terms of the general values of love, justice and mercy and devote more energy to their social implementation.

The third value of the secular school lies in the professional skill of the teachers and educators. Neither the Protestant nor Roman Catholic parochial schools on the one hand nor the church colleges on the other have become such models of educational perfection with respect to either secular or religious subjects as to make them exemplars for or critics of the secular schools. There is still much that the religious leader can learn from secular education in terms of skills, devotion to the truth and the use of critical study of one's own presuppositions.

Lists of the values found in the secular schools or a summary of the churches' share in responsibility for the secularism of our day is not likely to eliminate the Church–State controversy or mute the generalized attack on the schools. Edwin E. Aubrey, in his excellent book *Secularism: A Myth*, suggests that "much of the criticism of secularism arises from a habit of thought that is still in the grip of an idealist philosophy, which sees the moral and spiritual struggle of man as a conflict between the present and an imagined future." The secular mind, on the other hand, sees ideals "not as escapist projections of one's dreams, but as guides for better adjustment of one's living to conditions that lie beyond the immediate scene."[6]

Since even the Roman Catholic Church and certainly all the Protestant churches are unlikely to provide a parallel school system in which every child is given religious as well as secular education, the task of the churches should not be to create resentment among public schoolmen through generalized criticism but to promulgate the following principles:

1. The church must acknowledge the devotion to truth and love that motivates many secular-school teachers.
2. The church must witness to that power in the world which gives an assurance of ultimate victory and immediate strength to those who, while working for human welfare, have a commitment beyond ordinary human loyalties.
3. The church should recognize that faith is not strengthened by excluding competing ideas and unfriendly persons but by integrating secular knowledge and activity into conceptions of universal meaning.
4. Finally, churchmen have an obligation to appropriate and work affirmatively within the decisions of the Supreme Court. In the prayer and Bible reading cases, it said:

> *It is insisted that unless [these] religious exercises are permitted a religion of secularism is established in the schools. We agree of course that the state may not establish a religion affirmatively opposing or showing hostility to religion, thus preferring those who believe in no religion over those who do believe. . . .*

> *In addition, it might well be said that one's education is not complete without a study of comparative religion or the history of religion and its relationship to the advancement of civilization. It certainly may be said that the Bible is worthy of study for its literary and historic qualities.*

> *Nothing we have said here indicates that such study of the Bible or of religion, when presented objectively as part of a secular program of education, may not be effected consistent with the first amendment.[7]*

In view of this statement and the Zorach decision, it would appear that those churchmen who do not accept the constructive possibilities open to them are purposely misusing the word "secularism" as a means to secure their own particular establishment of religion.

PART II

---

*Practices
and Proposals
in Education*

5

Secular and Parochial Schools

Secular public schools and the parochial school system are comparatively recent experiments in human history. They did not, for example, exist in the Middle Ages. They do not exist today in much of the world.

In Colonial America both state and church schools flourished. The state schools included religious instruction and the church schools often received tax support. In 1827 the Massachusetts legislature, having to deal with a number of different religious sects, decided that textbooks could not be used in the public schools if they favored "any religious sect or tenet." It was sectarianism rather than religion as such that was to be avoided. The first impetus toward ending sectarianism came from Protestants, but the net result was a vague Protestantism that left neither the Protestants nor Roman Catholics very happy.

In looking for a way to continue a more vital religious education, Protestants turned to the Sunday school. Religious instruction on this model had existed before but without quite the same centrality it assumed in the nineteenth century. Protestants also began to explore weekday church schools such as the elementary schools the Lutherans in Pennsylvania established. In the 1840s the Presbyterians began to organize parochial schools and in New Jersey worked with little success to get public funds to support them. Faced with the difficulty of financing a system of parochial schools, the Presbyterians abandoned them about 1870.[1]

The Roman Catholic impetus to end sectarianism in the public schools and the establishment of parochial schools was far more successful. Because the public schools included religious practices and instructions that were largely Protestant in nature, the Roman Catholic Church was concerned about the unfavorable effect of such practices on Roman Catholic children. A Roman Catholic council held in Baltimore in 1840 directed priests to do what they could to eliminate these religious practices from the schools. In the course of their political efforts to establish a genuinely secular public school system, anti-Catholic hostility arose and Protestants rallied to the support of the public schools as they then existed. As a consequence, Bishop John Hughes of New York City tried to gain public support for Roman Catholic schools and, failing this, proceeded to organize Catholic elementary schools. He insisted that each priest appointed as pastor in the diocese of New York "proceed upon the principle that, in this age and this country, the school is before the church." The third Roman Catholic council held in Baltimore in 1884 endorsed Bishop Hughes's policy and decided that every pastor must establish a parish school within two years unless he was granted permission for a delay.[2]

After 1876 Congress required that every state admitted to the Union maintain a school system that was "free from sectarian control," but a Protestant religious tone continued in a number of states through Bible reading and prayer until the Supreme Court decision in 1963. In the twentieth century, Jewish groups have become active in attempting to eliminate religious practices from the public schools. Jewish, Protestant and Roman Catholic groups have all played a part in varying periods of American history in minimizing the religious content of public school activity.

Although education was originally intended at least to promote religion, it could not continue to do so in a religiously pluralistic and increasingly secular society. Shortly, the demands on education to train for economic and political careers largely supplanted training for religion as the rationale for education in American life. Nevertheless the Roman Catholics, the Missouri Synod Lutherans, and the Seventh Day Adventists still maintain religious education as the rationale for their weekday church schools.

The efficiency of parochial schools has been called into question precisely at the point of their major reason for existence. A study financed by the Carnegie Corporation and the Federal Office of Education revealed that the religious devotion of an individual's family was more important than formal education in influencing religious attitudes. The authors of the study, the Reverend Andrew M. Greeley, a Roman Catholic, and Peter H. Rossi, a non-Catholic sociologist at the University of Chicago, found on the basis of interviews and questionnaires that American Roman Catholics had a "high level of minimal allegiance" to their faith and that "the absence of a Catholic education does not seem to lead to a notable decline in minimal allegiance." The study also found that there is "no evidence that Catholic schools have been necessary for the survival of American Catholicism."[3] The July 26, 1966, Denver *Post* report of the study began with these words: "Education in Roman Catholic schools has been virtually wasted on three quarters of the students, so far as influencing their religious behavior is concerned. . . ."

Although there is no evidence that Roman Catholics are prepared to abandon parochial schools, there is some evidence of a willingness to experiment with part-time secular education. Shared time, or dual school, enrollment, which was included in the Elementary and Secondary Education Act of 1965, was endorsed by spokesmen for the National Catholic Welfare Council and the National Council of Churches. Dual enrollment would permit some parochial school children to receive part of their training in church schools and part in public schools or supplementary education centers. Some subjects such as typewriting, industrial training, mathematics, chemistry, foreign languages, could be taught in a secular program, whereas Roman Catholics seem eager to continue to teach history, the social sciences, biology and certain other subjects in parochial schools because of their religious or doctrinal implications.[4]

The Lutheran Church in America, which also operates parochial schools, has questioned the validity of such schools. That church's Board of Parish Education unanimously adopted a statement declaring that religious education is best provided in church and home and general education by the public schools. "In a pluralistic society," it said, "the state is the best equipped of all social institutions to insure that an opportunity for an adequate education is provided for all its citizens. . . ." The statement also said: "to ask the church to set up a system of education, even for its own members, in order to transmit culture and to guide the growth of pupils in the totality of their educational needs is to divert it from its primary task." The Lutheran Church in America operated sixteen parochial schools in 1963.[5]

Developments in secular and religious education and rapid social change have led to changes in both Protestant and Roman Catholic viewpoints with respect to education. Protestants on the whole tend to value secular education as having a validity of its own apart from religious education. Their reason for not operating parochial schools today is both financially and theologically based. In their view, secular schools like the secular world are to be affirmed rather than denigrated, for theologically, the world and time are not simply where God chose to be revealed but where He continues to be known. The task of the church therefore is to transform society rather than withdraw from it, to educate its children in secular rather than in separate schools. Most Protestants believe that both man's ability to reason and man's freedom have been given to him by God and that the ability to reason must be exercised in freedom. Given freedom within which to operate, reason becomes autonomous in the determination of its goals, independent of prejudice, dogma, or tradition.

It was not always so. Indeed, both Protestant and Roman Catholic churches historically have attempted to restrict free inquiry. The sixteenth-century church, faced with Copernicus' theory that the earth was not the center of the universe, forbade teaching the new theory "unless the teacher made it clear that he was presenting it as a purely speculative hypothesis and untrue in fact." Galileo's discoveries were "condemned as 'absurd in philosophy and formally heretical, because expressly contrary to Holy Scripture.'"[6] More recently, some Protestants and Roman Catholics have condemned the idea of biological evolution, solely on its seeming lack of harmony with the book of Genesis.

The mathematician, the physicist, the biologist, the social scientist, must be free to use reason as the means to determine the truth, so that what is discovered or learned is a reliable basis upon which to build further knowledge. The rules that govern the art of research, learning and experimentation not only are independent of faith but must necessarily be if they are to be objective. This does not mean that reason and faith are irrevocably separate, for belief is not possible without some ability to reason. Likewise, reason is not possible without some prior faith that the world has a rational structure. But man cannot learn to know God solely by reason. God is known through revelation, a process that involves man's ability to understand and grasp what God discloses to man. Secular education is based on reason and is primarily related to the mind of man even though it is also concerned about values and devotion to the truth. Religious education, on the other hand, is based on revelation and is primarily related to man's heart or will. Nevertheless it too must be aided by reason and sound scholarship.

Emil Brunner, the great twentieth-century European theologian, set forth a Protestant thesis that education is basically secular:

> Even the most highly educated person has just as much need of the divine grace and forgiveness as the uneducated and this forgiveness is not imparted to him through education but through grace. The Church is not an educational institution, but it is the community of the redeemed. . . . "Religious instruction" as it is wrongly called, has primarily nothing to do with education, but it is the action of the church. This holds good even when the church acts not through any kind of official representatives but through her members in the "priesthood of all believers." Even the father who prays with his children and reads the Bible with them acts not as an educator but as a "priest," not in the "world" but in the "church."[7]

This is to say that the performance of religious rites and the religious training of youth, however much they involve the forms of education, are the functions of the community of faith and are conditioned basically by the nature of faith and the broad or narrow interpretation of the revelation given. The general cultural, technical and professional training of youth is properly the function of the secular community. The secular community ought to be understood as a community of families and neighbors, a society as distinguished from a highly centralized state.

There are at least three reasons why general cultural as well as technical training is the function of the secular community. The first is that there is no such thing as a Christian mathematics or a Christian economic system or a Christian culture or a Christian nation. No political or economic system is identical with the Kingdom of God. The state, by both definition and function, is an agent of legal restraint and coercion rather than of unarmed redemptive love. Secondly, all culture, whether created by Christians or non-Christians, is created by sinners, partaking of economic and political power and partisan interests. The Christian community can make a contribution to the general culture in terms of witness and constructive criticism only if the church is not wholly identified with the culture as its author, educator and sustainer. In the third place, the church needs the criticism and challenge of secular education. If we believe that the Good and the True are both manifestations of God, then scientific truth is always a challenge to or judgment upon religious belief. Likewise, if we realize the dangers in the sinful application of scientific discoveries to life, then Goodness or Love is a necessary corrective to or limitation upon science.

The church cannot, however, yield to the temptation of secular society to regard scientific explanations of the universe as final. Scientific formulations at best provide a partial view of life. They are based on imperfect human interpretations of matter, else how explain different scientific theories or changes from Bacon's time to Einstein's. The conclusions of science must always be subject to continuing evaluation.

The essence of secular education is not a theory or conclusion such as atheism or naturalism. Rather its essence is the scientific method of investigation and critical evaluation, together with free communication among persons of different backgrounds and convictions. Secular education ought properly to abstain from the teaching of a particular religious doctrine or viewpoint, just as it ought to abstain from teaching an antireligious point of view. It can and should recognize the fact of religion, as well as differences in religious belief and practice, and maintain a friendly attitude toward the efforts of persons who hold or seek to discover religious meaning in life and its relationships. Secular education ought to be concerned about the objective study of religion and explore such questions as, What are the religious groups in our society? Why these particular groups? What impact have they had on our culture? These are valid topics for objective study. Secular education must also be concerned with character education and ethical values and hence with commitment to personal integrity, democratic values, critical evaluation of institutions and ideas and questions of international cooperation.

Roman Catholic, Missouri Synod Lutherans and Seventh Day Adventists take a different approach to education. Pope Pius XI in his encyclical "Christian Education of Youth" stated that "the only school approved by the Church is one where . . . the Catholic Religion permeates the entire atmosphere." No critical examination of Church dogma nor any teaching that conflicts with Church doctrine is permitted. Similarly "A Catalogue of Instructional Materials for Lutheran Elementary Schools" indicates that "a Lutheran elementary school teacher will insist that all areas of the curriculum reflect an adequate philosophy of Christian education. Thus he will select content and provide experiences that are consistent with such a philosophy."[8] The Seventh Day Adventist church says ". . . we do not rest content with offering courses in Bible and religion, but also endeavor to permeate all branches of learning with a spiritual outlook."[9]

Those philosophies of education that believe religion must permeate all teaching have produced a parochial school system. There is a further reason for parochial schools, however. Roman Catholic schools were started, as has already been suggested, to protect children from Protestant influences. The Reverend John McKenzie, S.J., indicated that "if we study the origins of the Catholic elementary school system, we discover that the prime motive of the founders was to protect the child from outside hostile influence."[10] Mary Perkins Ryan, an influential member of the National Council of Catholic Women, has written that in the "state of siege" in which Roman Catholics found themselves, parochial schools performed two functions: the first was that

> the faithful needed to be equipped with weapons of defense against the Protestant teachings which were opposed to Catholic doctrines. And so on the one hand, very little stress was put on doctrines which Catholics and Protestants hold in common, and on the other, the life Christ gives to His Church was not the object of much attention.

The second function was that of isolation. Miss Ryan wrote that "in a state of siege . . . those who cannot be adequately equipped to fight the enemy are to be kept safe inside the walls; every aspect of life needs to be under the direct control of the authorities."[11] The Oklahoma Courier, in an editorial by a Roman Catholic priest, suggested that John F. Kennedy would not have become President if he had received his formal education in Roman Catholic schools. Such institutions train leaders for Catholic communities and not for an American pluralistic society, the editorial said.[12]

Recent developments indicate that some Roman Catholics are unhappy about the "protective" function of Roman Catholic schools. In an address to 4500 parochial-school teachers and administrators in St. Louis in 1963, Father McKenzie said: "It is not the function of the school to protect the student against anything." He added: "All a school can do is teach, and this other objective—protection—spoils the goal of teaching."[13]

In comment on the decisions of the Second Vatican Council, Mary Perkins Ryan, in her book Are Parochial Schools the Answer?, insists that "the role of the Church . . . is now clearly not so much to protect as to communicate. . . ." She speaks of "freedom to find and serve Christ in our neighbor, no longer held back by fear that we may lose our faith in coming closer to that neighbor. . . ."[14]

These progressive voices are not the dominant voices in the Roman Catholic Church. Yet they seem to be speaking and writing in the spirit of the Second Vatican Council with all that it portends.

Any discussion of secular education sooner or later leads to questions of the role of government in education and the degree of governmental control over education. To what degree is education of children the right and responsibility of the parent or the church?

In a primitive pastoral or agricultural society, education is largely and necessarily in the hands of the family. Even in a highly complex industrial society the family is the full-time center for education during the early years of life. But society also has a stake in the education of children. In a complex industrial society, education in health, safety, public order, literacy and other skills that enable men to participate effectively in economic and political life is properly the concern of the whole community. Poor health and safety procedures or inability to participate in the economic and political life of the community may rob or endanger the whole community.

In such a society the only way to ensure that everyone has the benefits of education is for the government, serving as the legal agency of the community, to require it and see that schools are available for all. A far-flung educational system requires ample funds for its support and certain standards of education, health and safety. Only the government can raise the necessary funds and insist on adequate standards. The reason for taxing the whole community is that the whole community, including those who have no children, benefits from the education of all. The reason for taxing on the basis of ability to pay originates in the reason for the existence of government—to preserve order. Only an equitable distribution of the cost among the population can prevent the injustice that threatens the existence of order.

Government necessarily has to play another role in education. In a religiously pluralist society where millions of people belong to different churches and differ strongly in their religious convictions, and other millions belong to no church, some even objecting to religious emphases, the role of government must be nondiscriminatory in order to be just. The only way for government to be nondiscriminatory is not to invade the field of religion in the first place. In terms of education this means that government is not the agency to teach religion, conduct worship or subsidize religious institutions. Even if government could aid each religion equally there would be discrimination against the rest of the population. Government's role must therefore be one of providing secular education. There are also theological reasons for expecting government to provide secular education. As has already been suggested, government is partisan and coercive in nature. There is something inherently vitiating about using the coercive power of government to try to make men religious.

The role of the government in education is limited in a democracy by other educational claims such as those of parents, teachers, churches and other community organizations. To some degree school administrators and teachers are responsive to parent-teacher associations, to local school boards, to pressures of business, labor, veterans, religious organizations. One of the most important of the limiting factors is the whole apparatus that trains teachers and defends them. In schools of education conducted in both private and state institutions of higher learning a largely autonomous profession is in charge of teacher education. Accreditation procedures as well as pressures from professional teacher organizations play a role in defending the schools from unwholesome government interference.

These limiting factors do not serve as a perfect or complete check upon government. Yet it is still true to a considerable degree that it is the community that educates even while the state requires and finances education. There is a difference of opinion about who has the prior or natural right to educate children. Many Protestants would deny that any one segment of the community has a prior or natural right. They would recognize parents, community, church and government as all having a mutual interest and mutual rights. Parents have a right to send children to private or parochial schools. But the government does not permit parents to deny education to a child or send a child to substandard schools.

The Roman Catholic Church claims that natural law gives parents the right to control their children's education but also assumes parental inability to act effectively. The result is that the Church has tended to take over the rights of parents. Canon Law 1374 gives to the Church and specifically the bishop of the diocese "the right . . . to decide under what circumstance and with what safeguards to prevent loss of faith it may be tolerated that Catholic children go to such [secular] schools."

Parochial school policies have been determined by the hierarchy or by diocesan superintendents of schools rather than by parents. In 1951 a survey by Monsignor Carl J. Ryan showed only four dioceses reporting lay membership on their school boards. In March, 1964, *Sign,* a Roman Catholic magazine, reported that a survey of the 143 diocesan school systems in fifty states and Puerto Rico revealed that only 89 U.S. dioceses have school boards. Of these, laymen and women are represented on 26 diocesan school boards and 31 other boards are considering lay appointments for the first time. Only 4 dioceses reported the laity in the majority on their school boards. An article by Edward J. Sullivan in the magazine said the survey showed that the idea of lay representation is still experimental.

In the Kansas City–St. Joseph diocese, prior to the Vatican Council, no one was elected to the board. The bishop made the appointments to the nine-member board, which, as of 1964, included three laymen.[15] The former school board did not have lay members. One parent who frequently wrote letters to the diocesan paper about school policies complained that for a period of seven or eight years the diocesan school board "has never issued a statement, has never held a meeting open to the laity, has never even indicated that the laity may direct suggestions, criticisms or commendations about the parochial schools to it." He added, perhaps too caustically, "In so far as the school boards are concerned, one might believe that only the parents of public school children have the primary obligation to educate."[16] Since the Vatican Council the school board includes elected laymen who must be approved by the bishop.

In the Roman Catholic parochial school system the clergy in practice have had the dominant voice with some parental or lay participation.

With respect to the public schools there are elected school boards that share responsibility with professional educators for school policies. But Jewish, Protestant and Roman Catholic laymen and clergymen are in a position to make their voices heard and frequently do so. It is therefore evident that parents, teachers, the church, society and government all have long-standing claims and involvements in the education of youth.

Because of anti-Catholicism or an unusual loyalty to public schools, many Protestants have been unfriendly to parochial schools or the undemocratic features of some parochial school systems.

In spite of the questions many Protestants have about parochial schools, they should insist on the right of religious groups to maintain parochial schools as alternatives to the public schools for at least three reasons. The first of these is that parochial schools are a valid expression of religious and civil liberty. The second is implicit in the values of independence and competition. So long as there are independent rival schools public schools can always be measured against another yardstick. One of the useful services any private school system can provide for society is healthy experimentation and superior standards. The third is a cautionary reason. Although most Protestants are not moved to operate parochial schools, it should be clear that the future of Protestantism or Christianity is not dependent on dogmatic endorsement of the public schools any more than it is on private schools. Protestants are committed to the necessity of compulsory education but should never give uncritical endorsement to one system of education, whether public or parochial.

6

Religious Practices in Public Schools

Worship in the nation's schools, which has been one of the hall-marks of the general cultural establishment of religion, received a serious blow when, on June 25, 1962 and again on June 17, 1963, the Supreme Court of the United States handed down decisions affecting devotional exercises in the public schools.

The 1962 decision forbade the use in the public schools of a prayer sponsored by the New York State Board of Regents. The majority opinion, written by Justice Hugo Black, stated:

It is neither sacrilegious nor anti-religious to say that each separate government in this country should stay out of the business of writing or sanctioning official prayers and leave that purely religious function to the people themselves and to those the people choose to look to for religious guidance.

The 1963 decision, whose majority opinion was written by Justice Tom C. Clark, forbade devotional exercises in the public schools. At issue specifically were state laws that required and school practices that involved the use of prayer and Bible read-ings. The court noted that such "exercises are prescribed as part of the curricular activities of students who are required by law to attend school. They are held in school buildings under the super-vision and with the participation of teachers employed in those schools." A distinction was made by the court between such religious practices that were in the nature of state-sponsored worship and a "study of the Bible or of religion, when presented objectively as part of a secular program of education."

Both decisions evoked a flood of controversial comment. Jewish leaders were quick to hail the decisions. Rabbi Uri Miller, presi-dent of the Synagogue Council of America, national agency for orthodox, conservative and reform Judaism, commended the court for holding in the 1963 decision that public institutions should be free from "prayers, Bible readings and sectarian practices." The National Council of Churches and a number of Protestant leaders from the major denominations also expressed approval of the decisions. Methodist Bishop John Wesley Lord's statement about the 1963 ruling was representative of this viewpoint:

> The decision makes it mandatory for us to seek ways of relat-ing religion and education in the life of a child that shall not be by statutory decree. Unless Bible reading and prayer are performed in an atmosphere of religious devotion, often not possible in the public school, the very act may be profaned and secularized to the detriment of the pupil.

On the other hand, the National Association of Evangelicals, a fundamentalist Protestant group, criticized the ruling "as a sad departure from this nation's heritage under God." The Greek Orthodox Church and most Roman Catholic bishops also opposed it. A Religious News Service dispatch of June 18, 1963, stated: "U.S. Roman Catholic bishops and spokesmen have generally deplored the Supreme Court decision against public school Bible reading and recitation of the Lord's Prayer." The dispatch re-ferred specifically to Cardinals Cushing and McIntyre, to Arch-bishops Patrick A. O'Boyle of Washington, D.C., Robert E. Lucey of San Antonio, and Paul John Hallinan of Atlanta, as well as to the Jesuit weekly America. The same dispatch added: "Not all

Catholic comment, however, was critical of the Court's decision. In Chicago, a priest-professor agreed with the court's ban. . . ." Cardinal Ritter of St. Louis joined the St. Louis Church Federation and the Rabbinical Association in a statement pledging cooperation and respect for the 1963 decision "as the law of the land." The Roman Catholic Archbishop of Indianapolis joined Protestant and Jewish leaders in that city in a statement that said in part: "We strongly approve of the position of the court."

A survey of editorial reaction in 169 newspapers published in 115 cities located in 35 states and the District of Columbia was made by the Anti-Defamation League of B'nai Brith. Of the 169 newspapers 103, or 61 per cent, editorially supported the 1963 decision. The Anti-Defamation League indicated a substantial shift in newspaper opinion since the 1962 decision. A B'nai Brith survey of magazines was summarized in these words: "All in all, magazine reaction to the Supreme Court's decision was rather restrained as compared to the outpouring of angry words which followed the 1962 New York Regents' Prayer decision."

From a religious perspective the primary argument for devotional exercises in the public schools is that religion ought to permeate the public or corporate life of the nation and the place to begin is with children in the schools. Stated negatively, if there is no religious emphasis in the schools there will be a religion of secularism put in its place.

Other arguments were expressed. Some felt that many children would not otherwise be familiar with prayer and the Bible. Dr. John C. Bennett of Union Theological Seminary in effect took this position when he said: "If the Court in the name of religious liberty tries to keep the lid on religious expression and teaching both in the public school and also in connection with experiments that involve cooperation with the public school, it will drive all religious communities to the establishment of parochial schools, much against the will of many." Arguments such as these are in large part reactions to the abandonment of a cultural religious expression rather than a considered judgment about the nature of public prayer and worship.

Public prayer either in a classroom or at a football game does not by its very use confer any magical or miraculous benefit on those in the class or stadium. Prayer is an act of worship by a community gathered for that purpose. As such it is conditioned by the faith of those who worship together. A Christian community or a Jewish community that shares a common faith meets to act out who it is before God. Just as Christian worship without Jesus Christ falls short of its full meaning, so Jewish worship loses its real meaning if mixed with Christian symbols.

Prayers, such as the one suggested in the New York State Regents' formula, when reduced to a lowest common denominator of faith to be inoffensive to different religious groups become theologically inadequate. Prayers such as this, instead of making or keeping the public schools religious, become secularized in order to be used in a pluralist classroom situation. Those who argue that the absence of prayer in the public schools leads to secularism are in effect confusing real religious expression with the appearance of being religious. So-called nonsectarian religion is a nonbiblical, artificial faith that must, in the long run, constitute a grave disservice to religion.

The dilemma faced by those who advocate public prayer in public schools is clear. Failure to use a lowest-common-denominator prayer offends those whose approach to prayer is different from the one leading the worship. On the other hand, a lowest-common-denominator approach tends to establish as a new state-sponsored religion the residuum of religious belief acceptable to all faiths. As such it reduces prayer to public ritual and thus secularizes it.

Those who define secularism as the absence either of public ritual or nominal recognition of God by the state evidently see values in watered-down culture religion. Their cultural ancestors were the devotees of culture religion in the Old Testament known as worshipers of Baal. They merged a popular watered-down worship of Jehovah with a worship of Baal, who was identified with fertility and the control of nature. The distinction between such ancient devotees, against whom the prophets spoke, and the modern devotees is the dualism of the latter. The dualism is seen in the public advocacy of what inevitably is culture religion and the practice, privately and in church, of religion with a specific faith content.

A further theological problem is posed to the advocates of worship in the public schools. The worship of God is by nature a voluntary expression and must not be associated with the coercive functions of the state. Governments are by nature instruments of restraint, designed to enforce justice and to promote the general welfare. If governments, including public agencies like the schools, are permitted or asked to engage in the conduct of worship or other religious activities such worship will be meaningless by being either non-denominational in its effort to be neutral or be strongly influenced by the dominant religious group. Being unable, by its nature, to determine the content of religious expression, any political group in government, furthermore, must not be permitted to prescribe the forms of worship and certainly not indirectly to determine what is orthodox or heretical in religion. The ritualistic and doctrinal expressions of religious faith must be left to the church and the home if "free exercise" of religion is to be preserved. The task of government with respect to religious conviction is to guarantee free expression to those who wish to proclaim it as well as to those who object to any or all religious doctrines.

If government, either in alliance with a specific denomination or with Christianity or Judaism as a faith, tends to be identified with a particular religious expression, both government and the church suffer. The actions of Israel, Spain, and the Union of South Africa give sufficient evidence of the misalliance between the objectives of the state and its use of religion to support its policies identified as they are with the dominant religious groups in those countries. The danger is not only that religious faith in its totality, rather than in its specific localized expressions, becomes identified with the policies and injustices of political units but that state-sponsored worship of the God of all men may be used to hallow narrow nationalism. Such merging of the religious expression with cultural and even governmental activity mutes and obscures the prophetic religious criticism without which vital faith cannot long endure and as a consequence of which the best interests of the state are damaged.

In addition to these theological dilemmas, certain practical problems arise from the holding of devotional exercises in the schools. Surely the delegation of responsibility either for worship or for religious education to the public school (and also the parochial school) is an invitation to parents to neglect their parental religious responsibilities. It is similarly true that worship, conducted before a captive audience, often alienates those who see it as a coercive affront and denial of their private beliefs. There are subtle as well as obvious dangers here. It should be obvious, for example, that children, especially those in high school and junior high school, may become antagonistic to religion because of their exposure to meaningless or perfunctory worship in the schools. As a consequence, some children are turned away from and made immune to further exploration of religion just as in medicine a small inoculation tends to ward off any real encounter with a virus. Often, a child who might otherwise be expected to have a healthy religious encounter and an increasing devotion to a particular faith is alienated by the religious presentation of an over-zealous teacher. Other teachers can be equally damaging by simply mouthing the prescribed words in such a perfunctory way as to make a mockery of a developing faith. Such parodies frequently indicate the reservations of some teachers about participating in public school worship, as many are simply not qualified to perform religious functions or interested in them.

Beyond these practical questions there are issues of civil liberties. Some who have supported school prayers have said, as did the New York Regents, that a child doesn't have to remain in the classroom or assembly while the others worship. He may walk out or remain absent during the opening devotional exercises. But school children, as is commonly known, find it even more difficult than their parents to be different from their associates. In cases where parents tell a child to walk out or remain silent during devotional exercises, the child is caught in a situation where to be loyal to his parents he must challenge the pattern acceptable to his teacher and classmates. Such pressure upon children is an invasion of the privacy of belief which is essential to genuine liberty. Likewise, the assumption that public schools should conduct or permit the holding of worship services, thereby forcing atheists, agnostics or other objectors to excuse themselves as non-believers, is a violation of their civil liberties. Justice Clark in the majority opinion in the 1963 prayer and Bible-reading cases rightly observed that such an assumption "threatens their religious liberty by placing a premium on belief as against non-belief and subjects their freedom of conscience to the rule of the majority."

The Catholic Reporter, in discussing the civil liberties problems of the case in the light of criticism of the decision by the Roman Catholic bishops, recalled the controversy surrounding the Edgerton case of 1890 in Wisconsin. Here Roman Catholic parents with children in the public schools argued against the use of the King James version of the Bible as incorrect and incomplete, saying "that Catholics believed the Scriptures ought not to be read indiscriminately without the guidance of authorized religious teachers and interpreters." The editor noted that "the five judges of the Wisconsin Supreme Court (all of them Protestants) found unanimously for the Catholic petitioners. A similar decision was handed down by the Illinois Supreme Court in 1910 and again the plaintiff was a Catholic. "In other words," the editor observed, "it does make a difference whose ox is being gored."[1] The point the editor was making is that the Supreme Court decision was not a defense of a particular point of view but of religious liberty.

A few have tried to make the point that the 1963 Supreme Court decision invaded the civil liberties of the majority. They contend that the objections of a minority have made it impossible for the majority to practice their religion in the schools. Actually there is no majority in the United States when it comes to religion. Every religious group is a minority group. There is a Protestant majority only if it can be assumed that all Protestant denominations are in agreement.

The issue, even so, is not minority rights vs. majority rights, but individual rights. The Supreme Court said what the Constitution also says, that religion is not a matter to be settled by majority vote. Under the court decision both majority and minority groups may freely practice their religious faith but the state as such may not so practice; neither may religious groups under state sponsorship or with the assistance of government coercion impose their faith on others.

In a significant discussion on "Government and Prayer" in the December, 1962, *New York University Law Review*, Edmund Cahn pointed out that the Constitution presupposes not only a minority right not to be persecuted but a majority "right not to participate in inflicting persecution." The First Amendment "makes it ethically safe to belong to the majority. By separating church and state, it assures the rarest and perhaps the most excellent of all civil rights: the constitutional right not to persecute." This means that a Protestant in a heavily Protestant area may honorably belong to a Protestant church, knowing that Protestant worship services are not being inflicted on Jews or Roman Catholics who attend public schools in his vicinity.

There is a difference also "between the will of a majority and the right of a majority," as Robert Hoyt, then the editor of *The Catholic Reporter*, observed. Individuals have rights against the majority will. The majority doesn't need rights to protect it from the individual citizen. All individuals, whether in the minority or in the majority, have, according to the First Amendment, the right to be free from coercion in their religious belief and practice.

The 1963 Supreme Court decision led to some public proposals by both religious and political figures. The noted Roman Catholic bishop, Fulton J. Sheen, suggested to a congressional committee that in the event a constitutional amendment overrode the court decision the school prayer might be "the prayer that every member is carrying with him in his pocket—'In God We Trust.' Others might ask for more. One could hardly ask for less. I am asking only for a recognition."[2] The Illinois legislature passed a bill permitting the recitation of four lines from "The Star-Spangled Banner," including the words "in God is our trust." Indeed, some states, through their governors or other officials, announced their intention to ignore the decision, while others agreed to comply and still others, such as New York's education commissioner, stated that the state's policy permitting periods of silent meditation in public school classrooms was not affected by the decision.

During the Eighty-eighth Congress Representative Frank J. Becker of New York introduced an amendment to the Constitution to permit the use of prayers or biblical scriptures "on a voluntary basis, in any governmental or public school, institution or place." The proposed amendment also said: "Nothing in this Constitution shall be deemed to prohibit making reference to the belief in, reliance upon or invoking the aid of God or a Supreme Being in any Governmental or public document, proceeding, activity, ceremony, school, institution or place or upon any coinage, currency, or obligation of the United States." Then, after such a sweeping grant to government of the right to sanctify any political activity or ceremony with religious terminology, Becker added: "Nothing in this article shall constitute an establishment of religion."

Twenty-six congressmen joined Becker in offering the amendment, and Becker further persuaded some 90 sponsors of their own amendments to agree on his version. He won the endorsement of the House Republican Policy Committee and came within 48 signatures of getting the 218 necessary to force his amendment out of the Judiciary Committee. In response, the Boston *Sunday Herald* on April 26, 1964, editorially stated: "For the first time in American history a dilution of the Bill of Rights is being solemnly and soberly undertaken." During the course of public hearings, Protestant and Jewish opposition to the amendment was vigorous. Although Bishop Sheen testified in favor of it, the National Catholic Welfare Council urged "caution" and the Jesuit weekly *America* opposed the amendment, as did thirty-four out of forty-six other Catholic publications.

As a result of the seven weeks of hearings, congressmen discovered to their astonishment that most of the leading clergymen and the major denominations favored the Supreme Court decisions. The public became more familiar with the reasoning behind the court rulings and as a result the character of the mail received by congressmen began to change from the original deluge favoring the amendment that had been organized by its proponents.

Two years later, in the Eighty-ninth Congress, Senator Everett Dirksen (R., Ill.) proposed another Constitutional amendment to permit prayer in public schools or other public buildings. During the public hearing, Protestant and Jewish spokesmen opposed the amendment and the Roman Catholic Church did not take an official position. As a result there were Roman Catholic spokesmen on both sides of the issue. The Dirksen amendment failed to get the two-thirds majority required for passage. Again, in the Ninetieth Congress, Senator Dirksen proposed an amendment, which proposal said: "Nothing contained in this Constitution shall abridge the right of persons lawfully assembled, in any public building which is supported in whole or in part through the expenditure of public funds to participate in non-denominational prayer."

A number of religious and public organizations proposed programs in harmony with the Supreme Court decision instead of attempting nullification by a constitutional amendment. Some communities, for example, took seriously the statement from the 1963 court decision that objective study of religion does not violate the First Amendment. In addition to developing courses for the objective study of religion, other communities arranged devotional meetings in churches near schools, while others enlisted the cooperation of local radio stations for a similar period of worship to be shared by families at the breakfast table. Still other organizations have distributed devotional materials to children for their own private meditation when they attend school.

The idea of teaching religion in the schools has been proposed from time to time in different communities. Although the 1963 Supreme Court decision apparently validated the objective study of religion as part of a secular program of education, there are popular ideas about such teaching as well as other problems that ought briefly to be considered. Some think of religion in terms of their own religious doctrines. Others, recognizing that the teaching of doctrines of any particular religious group is impossible in our pluralist society, advocate non-sectarian religious teaching. This sometimes means that the traditions, beliefs and concepts that are common to Jews, Protestants and Roman Catholics should be taught, a common concept for example, being the Fatherhood of God and the brotherhood of man.

Difficulties with this position abound. As has been noted previously, any effort to seek a common denominator among various faiths inevitably leads to a dilution of the distinctive and really meaningful aspects of each. Certainly, the effort to teach religion-in-general leaves many ultimate questions unanswered, for as someone has suggested, everyone's religion is no one's religion. Finally, those who object to the teaching of religion as such have constitutional rights and should not be forced to submit even to what others regard as "inoffensive" religion, or to any attempt to teach religious courses "objectively."

Another proposal holds that religion should be taught in terms of moral and spiritual values. Those who object to such teaching object to the use of religious justification or theological doctrines as the basis for human value. However, it is possible to teach moral and spiritual values without religious justification and essential that teaching be conducted in this manner since invoking sectarian or theological sources for moral values would be a violation of separation of Church and State. But beyond this, Christians can endorse in Christian terms the statement of a Jewish writer who said:

> . . . *we are concerned lest the offering by the public schools of limited and inadequate religious education may result in its acceptance by many as a substitute for thorough religious education such as is afforded by the Jewish religious schools which the Jewish group has built and maintains.*[3]

In general there are two approaches to the factual or objective teaching about religion. The first involves religion as intrinsic to the subject matter of another course. It would be impossible to teach ancient and medieval history without discussing the origin, rise and impact on society of the Christian church, the Protestant Reformation, and the subsequent social and political events affected by religious men. Similarly the history or appreciation of art could not be taught without including the great religious art of the centuries. In general it is recognized that the role that religion has played in the development of civilization and in the life of men should be a part of the regular subject matter of the course where that role is relevant.

The second approach is to introduce specific courses about religion. On the college level, where students have greater maturity, state schools have found it possible to offer objective elective courses that treat the Bible as literature and analyze religious and cultural forms in courses on comparative religion or the sociology of religion. In public secondary schools such elective courses would be legal and feasible if taught objectively by personnel trained for such teaching. There is, however, no clear consensus even among religious groups concerning such classes. The Synagogue Council of America, for example, says that "factual, objective and impartial teaching about the doctrines of religion is an unattainable position." On the other hand, Arthur S. Flemming in his inaugural address as President of the National Council of Churches on December 3, 1966, urged that public schools undertake the task of objective teaching about religion.

Some communities give credit toward graduation for courses in religion tau.ght by church authorities to those who desire them outside of school time. Such arrangements avoid government subsidy of religion, for the school incurs no expense. They involve no danger of divisiveness or controversy within the schools, no subjection of nonreligious persons to the school's teaching of religion, and no discrimination. However, problems arise as to whether such credits are in lieu of other essential subjects in the school curriculum. If not, such credits may not be needed for graduation and student demand for them will diminish. Further, the public school cannot be sure, unless it supervises the teaching, that such courses meet the academic and professional requirements of the public school.

In 1931, in New York City, a proposal for such credit was dropped after the American Association for the Advancement of Atheism petitioned for the same privilege.[4] If various sects and pressure groups wanted to give such credit courses the problem of fairness and administrative assurance about academic standards would have to be very carefully scrutinized. It is worth noting in this regard that the Synagogue Council of America opposes the granting of school credits for religious studies.

It is necessary to be reminded that prayer and Bible reading are not the only religious observances that have been evident in the public schools. In many schools celebrations of religious holidays have been observed with special religious exercises, pageants or symbolic dramatizations of the faith. The celebration of Christmas and other Christian holidays is offensive not only to Jews and other nonChristians (as is also the case with celebration of Jewish holidays) but also to some Christians whose beliefs or interpretations do not coincide with those used. Religious faith is often so intensely and emotionally a part of each person's life and his family solidarity that contradictory emphases in the school are destructive and unsettling. A Jewish publication put it this way: "Christological observances in the schools may leave the Jewish child with no option other than to detach himself from his classmates and disbelieve his teachers or to betray family tradition and disbelieve his parents."[5]

The effort to combine Christian and Jewish observances as a

joint cultural expression has sometimes been suggested as a way to resolve the problem. It does not of course resolve it for non-Christians and non-Jews. It is even objectionable to many Christians and Jews. A member of the faculty of the Catholic University has raised "grave doubts about the propriety of such a joint celebration. On Christmas we celebrate the nativity of the Son of God. Can we really believe that Jesus Christ is divine, God Himself, and at the same time subordinate the observance of His earthly birth date . . . so as to make room for the observance, on exactly equal terms, of the story of Channukah?" [6]

If public schools are really neutral as between religious groups, then religious observances as such are necessarily excluded from the schools. On the other hand, schools can appropriately excuse students for the celebration in home, church or synagogue of major religious holidays significant to a given religious community. When the numbers involved are so great as to involve a large minority or a majority of students, it is reasonable to close the school for such a holiday.

The use in public schools of a crucifix, a nativity crèche or other distinctively religious or sectarian symbols poses similar problems to those involved in religious celebrations. They are offensive to those Christians who reject such symbols, to Jews and to those who reject religion, and refusing to display them in the public schools or in front of the school does not hurt religion. Their display is more likely to profane sacred things. Dean Kelley wrote:

> Who are the real "secularizers"? Those who want to take the holiest signs and symbols of the Christian faith out into the market-place to make the population be good! Far from achieving this laudable objective, the sacred symbols are themselves cheapened, degraded, taken for granted. And when they are dragged back into the sacred precincts, faded and worn and marred, they have lost their power to evoke reverence or inspiration even in those who revere them. [7]

Teaching in a distinctive religious garb or clerical attire is another form of religious symbolism. As such it may pose serious obstacles to relationships and learning on the part of some students. Such distinctive dress brings into the school a sectarian influence that introduces other problems. For example, Roman Catholic children might find it difficult and conflict-creating to address a garbed nun as Miss Jones instead of Sister Cecilia. It might also be difficult for a teacher with an out-of-school relationship to the same children, such as a Protestant pastor or a Roman Catholic nun, not to act as an ecclesiastical person or representative of the church, especially if there is no change from the clerical attire in his secular teaching role. On the other hand, clergymen and nuns when qualified to teach secular subjects should not be prohibited from doing so because of their ordination or commitment to the church. Qualification for public employment ought not to be determined by an individual's religious or political belief but only by his overt acts. It would be perfectly proper first to admonish and then to dismiss anyone, whether layman or clergyman, who tried to propagandize or proselytize for his sectarian beliefs or organization in the public school.

Other questions than those about religious garb present themselves in connection with clergymen and nuns who teach in public schools. May a person with a vow of poverty or one who asks that his salary checks be made out to his church or religious order teach in public schools? In such situations ought not the school to pay salaries, as is done to other teachers who have no such commitments? The member of the religious order should be able to contribute his salary to his church without penalty except for the income taxes required of any salary earner.

The baccalaureate service is another religious activity often taking place under school sponsorship and sometimes in school buildings. Almost universally Protestant, such services are one of the significant continuing indications of Protestant violation of religious liberty. That representatives of more than one denomination or faith may participate does not change either their essentially Protestant or religious nature. Serious conflicts of loyalty result as Roman Catholics have been forbidden by canon 1258 to participate in religious services of non-Catholics and Jews find Christian worship objectionable. Certainly Protestants would find Roman Catholic services or those of Protestant denominations other than their own to be a problem. Whether a baccalaureate service is conducted on school property or as an official school exercise in a church, it is hardly a proper activity of the public schools. A better way to handle the baccalaureate services is for one or more churches or the local Council of Churches to sponsor such services, inviting their own and possibly other students to attend.

Religious practices in the public school, which range all the way from daily prayer to such once-a-year activities as a Christmas pageant or a baccalaureate service, are an unnecessary offense to both Christians and non-Christans. It is, from the standpoint of the Christians, unnecessary because no evidence has been produced to show that a child's Christian faith is dependent upon or enhanced by such public religious ritual. It is no less an offense to those who feel that their children are captives, being forced to submit to a religious practice uncondoned by either their church or their parents.

Any religious compulsion denies the premise held by Protestants and Roman Catholics alike that genuine faith is always voluntary.

7

Tuition Grants to Children

A new source of friction has appeared on the Church–State horizon in recent years in the form of proposals for tuition grants to children in parochial schools. Government aid to parochial schools has been a long-time objective of many churchmen who have the responsibility of financing such schools. In the United States, constitutional provisions and the opposition of a large majority of Americans of all faiths have prevented the adoption of a policy of direct grants to parochial schools.

However, in the October 25, 1957, *U.S. News and World Report* the Reverend Virgil C. Blum, S.J., an assistant professor of political science at Marquette University, advocated a program of indirect aid to parochial schools which he called "the certificate or voucher plan." Citizens for Educational Freedom, which was organized in 1959 in St. Louis to secure aid for parochial schools, has endorsed and lobbied for Father Blum's plan. Although CEF's membership is almost entirely Roman Catholic, it welcomes others who support its basic aims. The *New Catholic Encyclopedia* describes it as believing that parents have the right "to choose the kind of school in which" their children "are to be educated." CEF "asks that any law passed to confer benefits on government schools be extended to private schools." CEF advocates various measures, such as public bus transportation to parochial schools, but its main thrust is Father Blum's plan of tuition grants, which he promotes through the slogan "freedom of choice in education." "Under such a plan," wrote Blum, "the State government gives parents of non-public school children certificates of money value for their children's education in the school of their choice." The child would present the voucher in September to his parochial school, which would redeem it with the state. In Missouri, CEF has asked for vouchers in the amount of $150 per child. In Kentucky in 1962 it asked for annual grants of $200 per child or an estimated $18 million per year. In New Jersey in 1965 CEF decided to ask for $250 per child for all children in both public and private schools at an estimated cost of some $394 million.

The tuition voucher plan has apparently received official Church support. In language reminiscent of that used by Father Blum and Citizens for Educational Freedom the Vatican Council Decree on Christian Education calls for public funds to be given to parents of school children. The decree, which was promulgated by Pope Paul VII, states:

> *Parents who have the primary and inalienable right and duty to educate their children must enjoy true liberty in their choice of schools. Consequently, the public power which has the obligation to protect and defend the rights of citizens must see to it, in its concern for distributive justice, that public subsidies are paid in such a way that parents are truly free to choose according to their conscience the schools they want for their children.*

The concept of distributive justice is the key to Roman Catholic thought about aid to parents with children in parochial schools. Ryan and Boland in *Catholic Principles of Politics* have defined distributive justice as

> *the duty incumbent on the State, conformably to its end and*

*purpose, to secure for each individual his right to a share in
the income from products he has helped to produce, observing
as far as possible the proportion which equity requires, to afford
him the necessary advantages and helps due him, and finally
to see that the public burdens and benefits are fairly and
equitably distributed.*[1]

The phrase "distributive justice" is an Aristotelian idea derived
from the concept that justice renders to each the rewards or pun-
ishments due him. Aristotle held that superior status or superior
contribution to society entitled one to greater benefits from that
society. It was an aristocratic principle which denied the benefits
of Greek citizenship to slaves. The medieval world in which
Roman Catholic structure, theology and social principles were so
largely formed was not fundamentally opposed to this idea of
distribution in proportion to status. Aristotle also used a concept
known as arithmetical justice, which gives the same equally to
each. In this way he narrowed justice into two categories: (1) distribution to everyone equally or (2) distribution by the same measure to persons unequally on the basis of status or previous contribution. The first of these is theoretically descriptive of the
American public school system, although that equality has not
yet been reached in many cities and states because of racial discrimination. The second category is the approach of private,
including parochial, schools. The demand for public funds for
those who, on the basis of religion or income or some other
standard, prefer private schools, is an effort to get distribution
of public funds to a certain class of persons.

The fact that a public school education is available to all without religious or class discrimination and in many states without
racial discrimination is not based in Greek thought but in Hebrew–
Christian thought. It is found in the Hebrew idea that man as
such is created in the image of God (Genesis 1:26) and the Christian idea that "there is no such thing as Jew and Greek, slave
and free man, male and female; for you are all one person in
Christ Jesus" (Galatians 3:28). It was modern democracy under the
influence of such biblical thought that insisted on the fundamental
dignity and equality of all men.

There are two facets to Christian thought about justice. One is
that everyone is of equal importance as a child of God. The other

is that men are unequal in their ability or understanding or contribution to society. Instead of distributive justice, which gives a man his due in terms of his contribution to society, Christian thought is concerned about redemptive justice, which gives a man his due in terms of his need. Emil Brunner, who described this concept of redemptive justice in his book *Justice and the Social Order*, cited Jesus' parable of the laborers in the vineyard (Matthew 20) as one illustration of Jesus' reversal of distributive justice. The laborers who worked longer received the same wage as those who worked shorter hours. Brunner said: "It is obvious that the parable is not meant to lay down rules for the payment of wages to laborers." Instead the parable reveals that redemptive justice "consists precisely in the cessation of all deserving" and is determined by the combination of man's essential worth to God plus his need.[2]

Distributive justice then is a pre-Christian and anti-Christian concept in that it makes a man's contribution the basis for his share in the public funds. Or as modern Catholicism uses the phrase "distributive justice," an individual has a "right to a share in the income from products he has helped to produce. . . ."[3] The Christian concept of justice, however, recognizes that distribution of public funds should not be based on what any man has contributed to the public treasury or public good but on human need. This would suggest that the neighbor in need, the poor and the minority, should receive a greater share in educational funds than those who are able to afford private school education.

The whole idea of distributive justice would probably not be advanced by Roman Catholic spokesmen if it were not for the vested interest in parochial school education of that church. Certainly the Roman Catholic Church does not defend distributive justice in terms of racial or minority relations, for this would argue for the *status quo* rather then compensatory education. Nevertheless, the unique Roman Catholic interest in parochial schools for its own children raises serious questions about the justice due the poor and needy in the public schools. The demand for aid to parochial schools or to children in them is never preceded by a demand for more funds for public schools and their underpaid teachers. As we shall observe later, CEF proposals would take funds away from the public schools. Distributive justice is thus a rationale for special privilege for a rival school system and hardly an illustration of Christian concern for the poor and needy of all faiths and none.

The whole notion of distributive justice is based on an assumption that certain parents as taxpayers are being denied justice if they do not get back from the government part or all of what they pay in taxes. Taxes, of course, are not levied on parents as such. They are levied on property and in some states on income or purchases. It is a matter of parental choice not to accept the benefits of public schools. But taxpayers without children have no choice of schools. They get no direct benefit from school taxes on their property. Does the concept of distributive justice mean that they should receive a tax rebate or some other reward? In an article in the September–October, 1964, *Liberty*, Floyd W. McBurney, Jr., summarizes the problem in these words:

> *No taxpayer has a right to demand that he get back as much as he puts in. If this principle were accepted, rich people would be able to claim the right to many more government services than poor people ever could. . . . Indeed, access to some government services, such as welfare activities, seems to have an inverse relationship to the amount of taxes a person pays.*

Both in theory and in practice, public schools benefit the community as a whole by lifting the level of education, skills and ability to participate in our democracy. No taxpayer without children or with children in private schools is deprived of the benefits of his tax dollars.

The Vatican Council Decree ties distributive justice and public subsidies to parental freedom of choice. Well before that decree Citizens for Educational Freedom, in its leaflet "Parents' Civil Rights in Education," asserted that "if government subsidizes the education of their children in one kind of school but not in another, parents have no freedom of choice." But freedom of choice to the average American has a different meaning than is implied by the CEF slogan or the Vatican Council Decree on Christian Education. Freedom of choice simply means that the government has not set up a monopoly in education or otherwise prevented the establishment of other schools. In the United States there are private and parochial schools as well as public schools. Similarly, freedom of association means that instead of having to belong to one government-sponsored association, individuals may form their own, unhampered by government surveillance. CEF and the Vatican Council Decree, however, assert that there is no freedom of choice unless government subsidizes an alternative to the public schools.

There are a number of problems in the freedom-of-choice argument which require attention and extended discussion, as do the constitutional questions raised, analogies drawn with the GI Bill of Rights and the economic problems associated with tuition grants. Each of these will be discussed as they apply to the problem. The question of freedom-of-choice has five facets.

1. The Constitution, whose First Amendment guarantees the free exercise of religion, prohibits government in the establishment clause from aiding or inhibiting religion. This means that under the free exercise clause anyone is free to form a church. But if it is argued that it costs money to build a church and poor men therefore have no freedom to exercise their religion in this particular way, it does not follow that government is obligated to build churches in order to guarantee freedom of religion. Freedom of choice or a constitutional right means that government shall not permit impediments to be put in the way of any citizen's exercise of his rights. It does not mean that the government must financially support any choice a man makes.

2. A parochial school is an integral part of a church. Parochial schools were set up by the church, are controlled by the church and exist for one purpose only—to provide sectarian religious education. The Vatican Council Decree says that the "proper function" of the "Catholic School" is "to order the whole of human culture to the news of salvation so that the knowledge the students gradually acquire of the world, life and man is illumined by faith." Since the Roman Catholic parochial schools and certain Protestant schools are adjuncts of the church, they are not independent agencies supervised by a group of parents or educators but integral parts of the church. The government's obligation toward church schools is therefore no greater and no less than its obligation to churches as such. Likewise, the government has no greater obligation to those who want to attend

church schools than to those who want to attend church.

3. Every citizen has the right to the religious education of his choice. But no person has a constitutional right to religious education at public expense. If there were such a right then freedom of choice would mean that citizens could choose to have their religious education on Saturday or Sunday or in the summer and expect the government to pay for it. If government were to give children tuition certificates only for religious education operated on a weekday basis, but not do likewise for religious education conducted at other times, the government would be discriminating in favor of one type of religious education and against other types. The only reason churches operate church schools as an alternative to public schools is to provide religious education; they would not operate secular schools solely to provide an alternative to the public school.

4. The argument of freedom of choice confuses church economic needs with legal rights. Parochial school education is becoming more expensive because of the teacher shortage and the costs of construction, supplies and equipment. Monsignor Thomas J. O'Brien, assistant education director for the Kansas City–St. Joseph Diocese has said: "We don't have the priests to start new parishes. We don't have the sisters to staff new schools. We don't have the money to finance them."[4] At one time parochial schools relied solely on the sacrificial living of underpaid nuns. "Now the odds are getting nearer and nearer to 50–50 that the teacher behind the desk is a lay person—earning a salary," said a survey of Catholic education.[5] All parochial school expenses must be met either by the church, by parents, or as is the case in some Roman Catholic parishes, by charging tuition. Other parishes, not charging tuition, meet costs through the contributions of church members whether they have children or not.

A survey of parochial school education in greater Kansas City revealed: "Half the parishes in Wyandotte and Johnson Counties in Kansas charge no tuition at all: The others range from $1 to $2.25 a month. On the Missouri side, eight parish schools charge no tuition. The others have a wide variety of arrangements."[6]

The diocesan high schools in the Missouri area have tuition rates running from $110 to $140 a year. "In Kansas the blanket tuition is $80 a year, an amount that must be subsidized by the feeder parishes. For example, the 19 parishes in the Ward High School District of Kansas City, Kansas, recently voted a $9000 subsidy, with the richest and biggest parishes getting soaked the most."[7] Since some parishes assume the obligation of school costs as a community of faith, the burden does not necessarily fall on those who are poorest or on those who have children. Those who contribute in this fashion have a tax incentive since contributions are tax deductible for income tax purposes whereas tuition payments are not. In these situations it is obvious that a tuition grant or certificate is intended to assist the church's economic plight. It is also clear that the parish makes the decision whether or not to charge tuition.

The effects of tuition grants are twofold. In the first instance, they will reward parents who now pay tuition to send their children to parochial schools. Secondly, they will affect those parishes that do not now charge tuition by bringing pressure to adopt that method in order to secure state funds, resulting in a reward or subsidy to the church.

5. The argument that without government subsidy parents do not have freedom of choice is belied by two factors. There are now 5,120,932 children in Roman Catholic elementary and secondary schools who could have gone to public schools.[8] Since World War I, private schools have grown faster each year than public schools.[9] These facts indicate that there are alternate systems of education for Roman Catholics and that millions exercise their right of choice without subsidy.

Actually, nonpublic education has grown steadily since 1900. That year only about 8 per cent of all pupils in elementary or secondary school grades attended nonpublic schools. The November 19, 1960, *Saturday Review* described the process as follows:

> By 1950 this number had almost tripled and represented nearly 12 per cent of the school population. By 1960 the number had all but doubled again and accounted for more than 15 per cent of the nation's total school enrollment. Thus from 1950 to 1960 while public school enrollments were increasing a phenomenal 43 per cent, in the nonpublic schools they jumped a whopping 90 per cent.

It is clear that as the nation's income and per capita income have soared, more and more private schools were created. However, in the United States in 1961–62, of the 5,736,480 who attended all nonpublic elementary and secondary schools, 5,120,932 children were enrolled in Roman Catholic schools. Obviously, therefore, the chief beneficiaries of any program of tuition grants would be Roman Catholic parents and Roman Catholic schools. Such figures reveal not only that freedom of choice already exists in the United States but that "distributive justice" is intended to finance a particular religious group.

Those advancing the program of tuition vouchers claim that "the certificate plan of direct educational grants to the individual child does not raise constitutional questions." Father Blum even suggests that "the certificate plan incorporates the same constitutional principles that underlie the educational provisions of the GI Bill of Rights."[1] Such an assertion ignores both federal and state constitutional problems such as those present in Missouri, typical of a number of states with strong and explicit amendments about Church–State and education. The Missouri constitution explicitly forbids the state and other public agencies "to pay from any public fund whatever, anything in aid of any religious creed, church or sectarian denomination whatever. . . ." Obviously, as the whole CEF effort is designed to obtain state money for the purpose of defraying parochial school costs, it runs directly counter to the provisions of the law. As George LaNoue points out, under the plan of CEF, the child would be "simply a conduit for getting tax funds to the private school."[12]

This proposal of tuition grants raises questions even in states whose constitution does not specifically provide for questions about Church–State and education. For example, in 1961, in *Swart vs. South Burlington School District*, Vermont was confronted with the question whether the state could pay tuition for pupils to attend a parochial school in a nearby town when there was no public high school in their own town. The Vermont Supreme Court ruled unanimously on the basis of the First Amendment of the U.S. Constitution that it was unconstitutional for a state to pay tuition for parochial school pupils. When the case was appealed, the U.S. Supreme Court refused to review the Vermont court decision, thus allowing it to stand. It did not, however, make it applicable to all other states. While this case is not identical to the CEF tuition grant proposal and therefore not conclusive, it further indicates that the profound constitutional questions about tuition grants for parochial school education cannot be lightly set aside.

Nor does the certificate plan parallel the education provision in the GI Bill of Rights. The GI Bill rewarded veterans with educational grants for service rendered to the nation, whereas CEF proposes tuition grants to children in no position to offer comparable service. The GI Bill was designed to enable men to resume their education in schools of their choice, after having their career plans interrupted by Selective Service. Obviously, children have not had their education interrupted by conscription. Furthermore, the GI Bill's grants enabled the individual recipient to go beyond basic education and encouraged the veteran with limited funds to secure advanced or higher training. The CEF proposal, on the other hand, is designed to encourage children to gain their education under religious auspices while ignoring the fact that educational opportunity is already freely available to all children. The GI Bill was not designed specifically to provide veterans with a private or church college educational alternative to free public education, since even state institutions charge tuition and other expenses on the college level. The motive for the GI Bill was not "freedom of choice" but encouragement of advanced study.

The chief supporters and the primary beneficiaries of tuition grants to children in private schools are parents whose children attend parochial schools and, preeminently, the Roman Catholic Church, which operates more than 90 per cent of the private elementary and secondary schools of the nation. The chief supporters and beneficiaries of the GI Bill were the veterans who otherwise would have had little or no chance for higher education. While enrollments at some church colleges increased as a consequence, this was incidental to the main purpose of the bill.

Citizens for Educational Freedom has also advanced an economic argument for state aid to children in parochial school. A presentation by CEF spokesmen included the following:

The Public Schools in Missouri are now receiving State aid

*through the School Foundation at the rate of approximately
$150 per student per year. We propose to ask the State to
extend this aid to the students attending private schools. As a
result of this move we expect that thousands of students would
choose to accept the offer and leave the public school system
to attend private schools. This would result in a large saving
to the public schools who would no longer have to provide for
the education of these children.*[13]

This argument is flawed by the fact that school districts also
receive other funds from local taxation. These taxes are not determined by a fixed subsidy per pupil but by over-all school
costs. For example, in a school building with 20 classrooms of
35 pupils each, 20 teachers, a librarian and a principal, were 5 to
10 pupils from each room to transfer to a parochial school the
costs of building maintenance, principal and teachers' salaries
would remain. Fewer pupils per teacher might mean better classroom instruction, but unless classes were to be consolidated and
teachers dismissed, savings would be few. Equally important so
far as the state is concerned, its cost of $150 per child remains,
whether he is enrolled in private or public school, affording no
saving to the state because a child is in one school instead of
another.

The hidden factor in the argument that the public would save
money by subsidizing those who attend parochial schools is the
assumption that parochial schools are less costly than public
schools. This is true only if less expensive equipment is used or
if teachers' salaries in parochial schools are substantially lower.
We know that nuns and lay teachers are paid less than public
school teachers, who are notoriously underpaid. CEF nevertheless
proposes that the public, in order to save money from public
schools, encourage a policy of transferring children to another
system with less than adequate equipment and at the expense of
underpaid teachers.

CEF, in seeking subsidy for those attending parochial schools,
tries to destroy the analogy of schools with certain other public
institutions. Because education is compulsory, "the choice of
schools in the education of children should not be compared with
such neutral functions of the state as public parks, highways,

police and fire protection and hospitals."[14] There is, of course, no need to use these comparisons. There are others. In every large state university there is a fully equipped university medical service, together with a staff of doctors, subsidized by the state and often by a required student's fee. Surely the state or the university need not be required to give each student a prorated part of the medical cost so that he may, if he prefers, go to a Christian Science practitioner or a faith healer and get a religious emphasis with his healing. Likewise, no one compulsorily enrolled under the Social Security system may expect government grants to enable him to secure old age insurance in a religious mutual fund if he prefers that to government social security.

Actually the comparisons with such neutral functions as police and fire protection are not illogical. Police and fire protection are compulsory. The city police and fire departments are *not* absolved from their duty of protecting life and property simply because someone hires a private detective or installs a sprinkler system. Public police and firemen exist not simply for the protection of the individual citizen or his property but to apprehend the criminal who may also attack others or to extinguish the fire that may spread to other property. If anyone feels more secure by hiring a private police service or private fire protection he is not entitled to any public grant or appropriation so that he may have freedom of choice of whom he wants to protect his property.

Finally, CEF seeks to discredit the public schools as "socialist" and in so doing uses a technique not unlike that of certain extremists. A CEF leaflet advertising a pamphlet, "Are Public Schools the Only Answer," states:

The American business community is actually participating in the drive to force school children into government owned schools and control, the nationalization and socialization of American education while at the same time hoping these youngsters will grow up committed to private enterprise and non-reliance on government.

In a similar statement Father Blum says:

The Certificate plan would moderate the trend toward the complete socialization of primary and secondary education; it would restore free enterprise in education.[15]

The implication that public schools are illustrations of nationalization is simply not true. The national government does not control public schools. The control is shared by the states and local school boards. American education can hardly be challenged as socialized any more than other services of the total community deserve the allegation. Functions of society that communities, states and nations perform, such as police protection, fire fighting, and sewage disposal, are not socialistic, nor are public agencies, whether a state university, a high school or the Coast Guard, fairly described by the term "socialism." Rather, the "socialization" argument of CEF more appropriately applies to their own interests, for parochial schools are hardly models of "free enterprise" in education. Not only are they not operated for profit, but they are not free in the sense that a group of parents may start one or determine its policies by democratic decision. The public schools, on the other hand, are managed by people who are chosen in a free election and are free also to choose their teaching faculty without religious discrimination.

There is a further reason why CEF's choice of the phrase "free enterprise" is unfortunate. Government subsidy of business is hardly free enterprise. If the lumber industry were having financial problems comparable to those facing parochial schools, and lumbermen, instead of asking for a direct grant to the industry, asked for government certificates to carpenters to be used to pay part of the cost of the lumber they need, government subsidy of the lumber industry as well as of carpenters would be the result.

What is really being proposed by CEF is a change in the American pattern of education—away from free public schools to state encouragement of parents to send their children to parochial schools that charge tuition—causing a shift from local control of schools to a system where education is controlled by sectarian groups under the administrative orders of a nonelected hierarchy. What CEF wants is not free enterprise. A private school is able to make some claim to the phrase "free enterprise" only so long as it is not dependent on government for its support. What CEF wants is government support of parochial schools without government control, or without such government restrictions as "no discrimination on the basis of race, religion or national origin in the selecting of faculty and students." In other words, CEF wants the cost of supporting parochial schools shared by those Protestants, Jews and nonreligious citizens who would be disqualified on religious grounds from teaching in or sending their children to those schools.

In conclusion, it must be observed that the problem of racial segregation is generally ignored by CEF in advocating tuition grants. In a number of large northern cities, private schools offer the only escape from planned desegregation of public schools and thus are growing rapidly through the transfer of children whose parents had not previously been very concerned about the values of religious education. Aid given to private schools by the state thus makes them more attractive havens for those who want to avoid racially mixed schools. Admittedly, some Roman Catholic schools are more integrated than some public schools, but others are not and there is an increase in the number of Protestant, Jewish and other private schools that are not racially mixed. It is one thing for private schools to determine their own policies with respect to admission of students and employment of teachers, but quite another to expect direct or indirect government support without public control. If through taxation the general public is expected to support an educational system, it should be a system that the public controls and that is nondiscriminatory.

In summary, the proposal of tuition grants for children attending parochial schools is a program of financial relief for those who are involved in paying for religious education in weekday schools. Its aim is to accomplish by indirection what cannot constitutionally be achieved directly.

At issue here is the specific purpose for which government funds are being sought—religious education. But also at issue is the highly questionable principle that there is no freedom of choice unless the government by taxation finances one specific approach to education chosen by one or more church groups. There are other methods of religious education that do not require government funds and do provide for freedom of choice.

8

Bus Transportation to Parochial Schools

One of the most sharply contested Church–State issues in the past two decades is that of public bus transportation to parochial schools. It has generally divided people along religious lines since its chief proponents are Roman Catholics and its chief opponents are Jews and Protestants.

Some Roman Catholics are known to be in opposition to any measure aiding church schools from public funds, but for the most part they feel impelled to remain silent. On the other hand, some members of a small fundamentalist Protestant sect, the Christian Reformed Church, have joined Citizens for Educational Freedom to work for various forms of aid for their church schools.

The issue therefore cannot simply be defined in terms of Protestant–Catholic rivalry. It is more accurate to say that, with one or two major exceptions, religious groups with a vested interest in weekday church schools have sought public funds for bus transportation. Of all the groups operating weekday church schools, the Seventh Day Adventists are the most consistent in vocally opposing public funds for bus transportation to parochial schools.

Bus transportation is an issue chiefly at the state level since it is state and local groups that authorize and finance bus travel to schools. The 1947 ruling of the Supreme Court in the Everson case left the decision on bus transportation to the various states.[1] The Everson case indicated that the federal Constitution did not prohibit the New Jersey practice of reimbursing parents of parochial and other private school children equally with the parents of public school children who rode to school on public transit buses. The decision did not deal with the renting or purchase of buses for parochial schools or with the reimbursement of parochial schools for pupil transportation. Since principles of constitutional law are established by what was actually decided in the case, Everson is hardly a reliable precedent for any and every form of public support of parochial school bus transportation.

The Everson decision was by a five to four vote. Justice William O. Douglas, who was one of the majority of five, indicated in *Engle vs. Vitale,* the New York Regents' Prayer case, that "the Everson case seems, in retrospect, to be out of line with the First Amendment." In other words, if Douglas were to have another similar case he would vote to overrule the right of states to reimburse parents for transportation to church schools.

The Everson case is permissive, not mandatory. Since many states have more restrictive constitutional provisions on Church–State matters than the federal Constitution it is state court interpretations that have been decisive. A number of state courts, such as Oklahoma's, Alaska's and Wisconsin's, have found that parochial school bus transportation is a form of aid to parochial schools.[2] Actually a majority of state court cases on bus transportation have been against the Everson decision.

The case for and against bus transportation to church schools has generally revolved around four major arguments. The first argument is that fairness requires that public funds be used to transport all children to school whether the schools are public or private, church or secular. Specifically this means that if the state decides to have public schools and the church decides to have church schools, fairness requires that if the state provides bus service to public schools it must also provide such service to church schools.

An examination of this argument reveals that advocates of bus service to weekday church schools are equating religious education with public or secular education. There are fallacies in this equation. The first is that religious education is not incidental to education in the parochial school. It is the only reason for having church schools.

The Vatican Council Declaration on Education asserts that the "proper function" of the Church in the field of education "is to create for the school community a special atmosphere . . . to help youth grow according to the new creatures they were made through Baptism . . . and finally to order the whole of human culture to the news of salvation. . . ." This means that there is only one reason for operating parochial schools—to provide sectarian religious education. In a secular state the state has no obligation to help finance church schools or transportation to church schools. In fact, it has an obligation not to support parochial schools because such support would discriminate against those who do not subscribe to weekday religious education.

As indicated earlier, most churches and synagogues in the United States provide religious education for their children on Saturdays or Sundays and in summer schools and conferences. Some provide religious education after school or on a released-time basis. If bus transportation were provided only to those churches that operate weekday church schools there would be discrimination against those churches that operate church schools on Saturday, Sunday and during the summer.

If bus service to parochial schools were paid out of public funds, Protestants, Jews and the unchurched would be forced to pay for bus transportation to Roman Catholic and other church schools as well as bus transportation to public schools. In addition, they would have to provide transportation at their own expense for their children to go to their own church schools. They would be forced to pay for buses for religious education of another religious group while being denied public bus transportation to their own type of religious education.

In 1965 the wife of the manager of the St. Louis Cardinals told a Missouri legislative committee that fair play in sports meant that no one on the team was left on base because of his race or religion. The same witness then suggested that fair play similarly would lead to the granting by the state of Missouri of public bus transportation to parochial school children. A careful examination of this analogy reveals that the witness was not asking fair play for all children but special privilege for one religious group. A more accurate analogy would recognize that the legislature is an umpire in a league with many different teams. If the legislature is to be an impartial umpire it will not assist a Roman Catholic team at the expense of a Jewish or Methodist or Presbyterian team.

One person testifying before a state legislative committee insisted that fairness and impartiality among religious groups would require that the following amendment be inserted in the parochial school bus bill:

> *When transportation is provided by a district to any parochial school which provides religious instruction or worship, the district shall without discrimination also provide transportation to all other church schools including those which conduct educational programs on Saturday, Sunday and during the summer.*

When seen in this light, proposals to finance transportation to parochial schools are intended to establish one type of religious education over all others as valid for tax support and, if adopted, would be the beginning of an establishment of one religion over another. In other words, the net impact of parochial school bus legislation would be serving the interest of the one or two religious groups that operate an extensive weekday system of church schools. Justice and fairness require a nondiscrimination policy with respect to all religious groups and the unchurched as well.

A second argument used to justify public buses for church schools is safety and health. During at least one state campaign to get public funds for parochial school bus transportation Citizens for Educational Freedom distributed a leaflet entitled "School Bus Safety for Children." It described the death of a mother and six children killed in Minnesota in 1959 "when their station wagon was struck by a fast freight train" while they were en route to the Sacred Heart School. The leaflet referred also to health by describing "a young boy and his sister, with noses running and cheeks lashed by bitter winds" who were "trudging along dangerous highways teeming with roaring horsepower." They were victims "of the political intrigue that prevents them from enjoying the comfort and safety of a school bus ride." This leaflet argues that bus service for parochial schools "is needed to protect the lives of our school children who now attend independent schools."

On the surface, this is a cogent argument. The state has a duty to protect all children. The real question is the purpose of school buses. Are they provided for public schools for safety reasons? Or for child welfare purposes? The answer clearly is no. Buses are not provided for school children who have to cross dangerous intersections en route to school if they live within walking distance of the school. Distance, not safety, is the reason for school buses.

In the days of the neighborhood school and before the time of school buses, everyone walked. When bus transportation became available, it was possible to build schools to serve a wider geographical area. School districts could save money by building consolidated schools. So they built fewer and better schools. The school bus that made this possible is therefore a direct benefit to the school rather than a safety measure for children.[3]

If bus transportation were a safety measure in the same sense that police and fire protection are safety measures, then bus transportation should be provided for children en route to churches, theaters, circuses, zoos and other places, just as police and fire protection are provided for children en route to these places and while they are in them.

Likewise, if school buses were the answer to child safety problems, then each child attending school should be picked up at his home. About two-thirds of all children enrolled in schools walk or otherwise reach school without benefit of school buses. These children are subject to the hazards of the road on each school day. In a large midwestern city, for example, a six-year-old girl, Lori Curry, was killed in 1965 and another six-year-old child, Teresa Wicklund, was killed in 1964. Both girls lived only a short distance from school and were walking to school. None of the advocates of parochial school bus transportation, however, has expressed an interest in having school buses pick up all public school children at their homes in order to guarantee their safety.

School buses as such do not guarantee safety. The *National Parent Teacher* Magazine for February, 1959, pointed out that "every year many pupils are injured, thirty or more of them fatally, in some 5,800 school bus accidents." In the state of Missouri in 1963 there were 307 school bus accidents, 190 of them involving collision with other vehicles. Of the 171 persons injured or killed 86 were school pupils.[4] No records are available in Missouri for the number of school children injured or killed while en route to school as pedestrians. But the neighboring state of Kansas, in the latest year for which such statistics were available, 1958–59, showed a total of only 40 accidents wherein a motor vehicle collided with a pedestrian between the ages of five and nineteen. These statistics do not prove that it is always safer to walk than to ride a school bus. They merely demonstrate that school buses are not necessarily a guarantee of safety.

When a school bus collides with another vehicle or some other obstacle, there is greater likelihood that a number of people will be injured simply because there are many pupils riding the bus. The Kansas City *Times* of October 23, 1965, reported, for example, thirteen injuries among 460 students riding in three school buses. The buses, which were escorted by a Johnson County sheriff's patrol car, crashed into each other when the lead bus struck the rear of the patrol car as it suddenly stopped.

"In Los Angeles on the afternoon of September 30, 1957," according to a report in the February, 1959, *National Parent Teacher,* "twenty-seven happy little children were going home on a parochial school bus when the bus lurched off a road . . . somersaulted thirty-five feet down a steep embankment and landed upside down in a rocky ravine." Five children between five and eight years of age and the driver were killed and 22 others were injured. The brakes were defective. In a dispatch from Bethel, Connecticut, on December 7, 1965, *The New York Times* reported: "A school bus carrying 62 pupils sideswiped a tree and overturned here about 8 A.M. today injuring 37 pupils and the woman driver." The National Safety Council reported 3700 children injured in bus accidents in 1964, a 75 per cent increase over 1960, although the number of children riding school buses increased only 40 per cent in the same period.

The school bus safety problem is of sufficient concern that in

1965 the National Safety Council cosponsored a research project with the University of California at Los Angeles to develop basic information for use in preparing safety specifications for school buses.[5]

It is also difficult to believe that churches that provide school buses for their parochial schools would be so insensitive as to provide buses only for some of the school children, those living at a distance, if safety and health were the real reason for buses.

Bus transportation, in other words, is not a health measure. Neither is it a welfare measure. Such transportation is not provided for children for any other purpose than education. Children are not given free bus rides to any other place, however great the distance or however hazardous the route. The purpose of bus legislation is to provide an educational service.

The implication of the leaflets and arguments of Citizens for Educational Freedom is that there is discrimination against parochial school children on the crucial matter of safety. The CEF leaflets never report that Protestants and Jews have been killed while en route to their church schools. Actually, there is no discrimination on religious grounds unless the state or a school district provides bus transportation to some church schools and not to others.

A third argument advanced in behalf of public bus service to parochial schools is that parochial schools perform a public service in that they educate school children and thus relieve the public school of that burden. The counterargument of course is that this is not the purpose of church schools. Church schools exist only to provide sectarian religious education. If sectarian religious education can be interpreted as a public service entitled to tax support, so also can churches as such be interpreted as performing a public service in reducing crime, alcoholism and the like.

The idea that parochial schools perform a public service can be used for more than the securing of bus transportation. There have been reports from states where parochial school transportation has been provided that the following argument has been used: "Look! You've admitted we are really public schools by giving bus transportation! Now give us the money for salaries for teachers!"[6]

Justice Brennan of the U.S. Supreme Court, a member of the Roman Catholic Church, defined "public function" in terms other than those used by advocates of government aid. They indicate that since churches educate those who would otherwise have to be educated in public schools the churches are performing a public function. In *Abington School District vs. Schempp*, Justice Brennan wrote in a concurring opinion:

> *It is implicit in the history and character of American Public Education that the Public Schools serve a uniquely public function; the training of American citizens, in an atmosphere free of parochial, divisive or separatist influences of any sort— an atmosphere in which children may assimilate a heritage common to all American groups and religions.*[7]

The test of whether parochial schools perform a public as distinct from a sectarian purpose is of course their willingness to accept the same responsibilities as public schools. If it is unlawful in public schools to discriminate on the basis of race or creed, and if it is unlawful to have religious observances sponsored by public schools, then any church school that claims the same rights to the public treasury should accept the same responsibilities. Similarly, no religious insignia, emblem or object should be displayed in any school that receives public funds. No church would accept such a nonreligious stance or such a nondiscriminatory role for either its teaching staff or its pupils.

There is another sense in which some parochial schools discriminate and hence are not serving a public purpose. The children of economically deprived parents do not have the money to pay for tuition to weekday church schools. They go to public schools. It is parents from the middle and upper classes, who can afford to send their children to parochial schools, who would benefit from publicly supported parochial school bus transportation.

Sometimes, proponents of public bus service to parochial schools assert that such bus transportation is necessary for religious freedom. If a parent cannot afford to send his children to a church school he does not have real freedom. The speciousness of this argument is seen if we ask whether a person is robbed of religious freedom if he cannot afford transportation on Sunday morning to the church of his choice.

The argument needs to be reversed. If parochial or other private schools are to remain free they should be privately supported. To accept tax funds is to accept some degree of public control and hence to lose independence. Otherwise there would be taxation without representation. Citizens who pay taxes for public schools have some control over school policy through elected school boards. If their taxes are used for private schools why should they not expect similar representation in determining school policy?

The nature of parochial school bus legislation is exposed if we use an analogy. The State has provided public schools for everyone just as it has provided certain other public services. Any citizen who does not like a public service such as a public highway or a public swimming pool may provide his own private highway or pool or join with others to provide such private services—at his own expense. Similarly, the parent who chooses not to send his children to the public school should expect to pay the cost of the private school of his choice, including transportation to it.

The fourth argument for providing bus service to parochial schools is the "child benefit" theory. This is simply the idea that it is the child and not the school that benefits. If the state declared it in the public interest to provide socialized bus transportation for all children through eighteen or nineteen years of age so that they could ride free to school, church, the zoo, theater or the homes of their schoolmates, there would be no Church–State problem, no problem of discrimination in favor of one form of religious education and no problem of aid to the school. But a "child benefit" program that is intended to aid children only at the point of private or parochial schools is suspect. It is not the child but the church school benefit that is uppermost.

The school bus law in Kansas sheds some light on the total problem. It was apparently an effort to compromise so that transportation would be provided but not to parochial school destinations. The legislation authorized transportation of private school pupils if they are picked up en route and discharged en route or at the public school destination. This applies in cases where school buses are owned by the public school district. Apparently the legislature reasoned that the public is responsible for transportation of any child of school age to a public school whether or not in fact he is enrolled in that school. The counterposition is that the public school is under no obligation to transport children to the public school who are not in fact enrolled in public schools. If the state were to adopt the "child benefit" theory as such, instead of aiding parochial schools through bus transportation it would provide every child at all times with free transportation on any bus line operating in the state.

The problem of parochial school bus transportation must be viewed also from another perspective. According to the August 23, 1964, South Bend, Indiana, *Tribune*, David La Driere, the national executive director of CEF, "indicated school bus laws are now a favorite opening wedge of CEF at the state level in securing tax support of private and church schools." The bus issue is thus in many respects simply an aspect of the whole effort to have the state support church schools.

9

Dual School Enrollment

One of the proposals advanced as a way out of the Church–State controversy in education is "dual school enrollment" or "shared time." About 1917, Walter Scott Athearn, who taught religious education at Boston University, developed a Malden, Massachusetts, Plan, which envisioned a city-wide program of weekday religious schools which would "share" the child's time with the public school. Under his plan, thoroughly competent teachers and facilities for the religious schools would supplement the education received in public schools.[1]

In the 1950s and 1960s the basic features of this plan were adopted to a new set of circumstances by a few Protestant leaders whose motives ranged from finding a way to protect the public schools from the parochial school lobby to concern for parochial school children who were being denied certain educational advantages. The educator most prominently associated with and favorably disposed toward the concept of dual enrollment is Harry L. Stearns, superintendent of schools in Englewood, New

Jersey, and a member of the United Presbyterian Board of Christian Education. He wrote that dual enrollment

> *in theory would remove the argument that parochial schools should be reimbursed for doing the State's job, for parents would be able to claim from the full offer of the public school that portion which they assume to be the State's job, and to obtain from their own or the church's expense only that portion of schooling which is determined to be of such religious import that it cannot be intrusted to lay or public authority.*[2]

In another article Stearns wrote: "It should help to relieve or eliminate the divisive argument for public funds for church schools."[3]

The concept of dual enrollment has been in practice for many years in Hartford, Connecticut, and a number of other cities. It allows parochial school pupils to attend a public school part-time to receive instruction in subjects that church authorities acknowledge are neutral or nonideological in content. These generally include business and vocational training, which require expensive equipment and laboratories, and often include physical education. Parochial schools usually reserve for themselves both religious education and such courses as history, literature, social studies, government and biology, which influence pupils in their attitudes and social values.

Dual enrollment differs in at least four respects from "released time," which has been widely adopted by religious groups in the United States. Under dual enrollment the parochial school is usually the institution of primary enrollment where records are kept and which awards the high school diploma. Under released time the public school is the institution of primary enrollment and the pupil is released on the parent's request for religious education classes during school hours when there is no educational conflict. Secondly, dual enrollment presupposes the primary interest of the church, which, through the church school, rather than by action of the parent, enrolls the child part-time in public school and prescribes the courses to be taken. The parochial school therefore maintains the primary relationship to the child and the parent. Released time presupposes a primary interest of the parent, who makes arrangements directly with the public school and with the church or teacher of religious subjects.

In the third place, dual enrollment provides academic credit for courses in religion or those taught from a religious perspective, whereas released time is for noncredit religious instruction. A fourth difference is that dual enrollment presupposes the existence of a parochial school with an extensive teaching staff, whereas under released time arrangements, it is possible for any church to participate in religious education under the leadership of a pastor or trained lay teacher without having to operate a parochial school.

The concept of dual enrollment or "shared time" rests upon two basic assumptions. It assumes the existence of a parochial school to which the parents prefer to send their child for part of his school time. It further assumes that children have the right to part-time enrollment in a public school if they meet the balance of their compulsory attendance and educational requirements in a nonpublic school. Neither assumption is broadly accepted and the second has been tested in Missouri, where the school law, upheld by the state Supreme Court, requires full-time attendance at one school.

The educational arguments against dual enrollment can readily be stated. Simply because a child or parent does not like the way a subject is taught he has no right to leave the public school for one or more classes in another school, and attend at the public school only such courses as he elects. There are two reasons for this. If such an option were exercised by any substantial group of pupils it would not only pose serious schedule and discipline problems but would deny an integrated educational experience to the child. The chaotic effect on the child would be profound were the argument's logical extension be made that if a child may attend more than one school he can attend more than two. The assumption behind dual enrollment is of course that a total school experience is not necessary for the child, but various studies of educational theory and method clearly indicate that by stressing individual classes the needed integration of a child's learning experience is denied. A government report lists as one of the disadvantages of shared time the fact that it "would permit neither public nor parochial schools to achieve a desirable correlation within the whole curriculum, as it would be divided between one school and another. In each school the curriculum would be narrowed from the viewpoint of comprehensiveness of all subject areas."[4]

Indeed, a Roman Catholic educator, Monsignor Eugene J. Malloy, superintendent of schools for the Diocese of Brooklyn, New York, told the National Catholic Education Association that "duplication of the learning environment, especially for young children, and especially for children already disadvantaged, will lead to educational loss rather than educational gain."[5]

Whatever the effect on the child, genuine legal and constitutional problems are posed. A New York attorney has stated the legal case in these words:

> *The child attending the religiously segregated school has the same right to attend the public school. But if he elects to secede from the public school he has no right to partially secede. Although the law guarantees the right of the religious child to withdraw from the public school, the same constitution forbids the state to give, or aid him in securing, the religious indoctrination he desires. Shared time is an indirect, if not a direct, support of religious indoctrination. It has the avowed purpose of promoting the growth of a competitive school system.*[6]

A federal government study of "shared time" poses some of the implied constitutional problems by stating:

> *Relatively little consideration has been given in the [current published] literature to shared time arrangements between public and nonpublic schools other than Catholic parochial schools. This is probably due to the facts that (1) all other nonpublic elementary and secondary schools together constitute only about 10 percent of the total number of such schools; (2) the other religious bodies operating the largest numbers of such schools have not been asking for Federal aid for them and have generally been represented in expressions of opposition to Federal financial aid to sectarian schools; and (3) operators of non-*

sectarian private schools have shown . . . relatively little interest in the controversy over Federal aid.[7]

From one point of view it can be asserted that no direct monetary appropriation goes to parochial schools. If, therefore, a parochial school benefits from the technical and physical facilities of public schools, including their classrooms and teachers, there is no violation of constitutional prohibitions. But from another perspective the dual enrollment plan has the specific objective of alleviating the financial burden of parochial schools in order to secure the support of church authorities for public schools. Philip Kurland, a professor of law at the University of Chicago and editor of the *Supreme Court Review*, stated that he considered

unconstitutional aid by way of shared time, which is the major form of relief afforded parochial schools by the 1965 legislation. For as I see it, there is no rationale for dividing pupils between public and private schools in the manner that most shared time programs would do except to relieve the financial burden of the parochial school.[8]

Although some Roman Catholic educators have shown an interest in shared time, Protestant hopes to eliminate public funds for church schools through the establishment of dual enrollment provisions have proved to be illusory. The proposal for dual enrollment was embodied in the Elementary and Secondary Education Act of 1965 with this objective in view and was likewise intended to resolve the impasse arising from the Roman Catholic hierarchy's refusal to let Congress approve general aid to public schools for teachers' salaries and school construction.[9] However, the Roman Catholic hierarchy has rejected the assumption of Protestant proponents of shared time that the adoption of dual enrollment would put an end to demands for public funds for parochial schools. Indeed a survey of existing dual school enrollment programs made by the U.S. Office of Education states:

Dual enrollment was not considered by school officials of the Archdiocese [of Detroit] as a substitute for possible direct Federal, State or local financial aid to education in archdiocesan schools. Nor was dual enrollment considered by them to be an adequate substitute for the full-time education of a Roman Catholic child in a Roman Catholic school. Archdiocesan school officials maintained their conviction of the desirability of both of these principles.[10]

The Second Vatican Council's Declaration on Education supports this thesis by noting that "the duty of educating belongs to the Church" and by asserting that "the public power must see to it, in its concern for distributive justice, that public subsidies are paid out in such a way that parents are truly free to choose according to their conscience the schools they want for their children." This position was put into political action in Michigan in February, 1968, when a bill was introduced in the Michigan legislature to provide tuition grants for children in parochial schools. The February 1, 1968, Flint, Michigan, *Journal* stated: "Catholic laymen received specific instructions Wednesday night on how to campaign for state funds to ease the financial problems of parochial schools."

Citizens for Educational Freedom, which wrote the tuition grant bill, has criticized dual enrollment. The Ohio CEF is on record as saying: "as long as direct participation in the benefits of educational tax funds is conditioned upon attendance at a public school, whether such attendance be permitted on a part-time basis, unjust financial coercion is the result."[11] Such claims lead inevitably to the position of a Roman Catholic educator serving on the Fordham University faculty. In response to the question "Is [dual enrollment] likely to be a permanent solution or a temporary one?," he said: "If parochial schools ever were to get sufficient federal aid, shared time would probably fade away."[12]

Leo Pfeffer, the constitutional lawyer of the American Jewish Congress, notes:

The Catholic Church has given no indication that it would cease its demands for inclusion of parochial schools in a Federal-aid program merely because [of dual enrollment]. . . . There is in fact no reason to expect that it would do so; it is far more likely that it would continue to press its demands. The net re-

sult would be to impose additional financial burdens upon the public school system rather than to ameliorate its crucial needs.[13]

One reason the Church does not solve the parochial school financial problem is its failure to provide a solution to both elementary and secondary school finances. Since "shared time arrangements are not feasible for elementary schools in which all subjects are frequently taught a particular class or grade by a single teacher,"[14] only the secondary parochial school sector would have its financial burden alleviated.

Roman Catholic leaders who testified at public congressional hearings prior to the adoption of the Elementary and Secondary Education Act of 1965 went along with the concept of dual enrollment. Monsignor William McManus said that "we feel now, as we did at the time of the Federal impact legislation, that we must go along, even though the benefit to us is extremely limited, in the interest of taking care of these desperately poor children in both metropolitan and rural areas."[15] During the testimony no indication was given of any willingness to settle for shared time as a solution to the Church–State problem. Instead, given the assumption of a dual enrollment system, Monsignor Frederick G. Hochwalt significantly reiterated the hierarchy's position of blocking bills that would aid public schools only.[16] It is clear therefore that future general aid to public schools must be dependent upon additional aid to parochial schools beyond that accorded through shared time, if the Church is to support aid to public education.

If the primary or only reason for shared time is to provide a solution to the problem raised by Roman Catholic demands for public funds, and if the Roman Catholic Church refuses to accept it as a solution, it would be a serious mistake to force it on the public school system.

Since the dual enrollment proposal originated as a method of resolving the problem of aid to parochial schools it was assumed that a genuine solution of that problem would be advantageous to the public schools. Very little consideration, however, was given to its over-all impact on public education. A number of serious consequences are likely to flow from a widespread acceptance of shared time. These include both academic and administrative consequences. One academic result is that an emphasis on dual enrollment tends to shift the role of the public schools from teaching for participation in a democracy to training for occupational proficiency. Shared time

> opens the door to a new philosophy of public education in which the public schools are to provide vocational training to all, but academic training only for those who do not attend parochial or private schools. This will . . . turn an increasing portion of the public school program to vocational training, with the academic subjects becoming an increasingly minor concern. . . . The private and parochial schools, in the meantime, will be free to put the bulk of their budgets into the academic areas. When these two tendencies run to their inevitable ends, it will be only the parochial and private schools which can give proper attention to the academic disciplines. Students desiring the best will thus be under pressure to leave the public schools for the parochial and private schools, and the students who cannot financially make the change will be left at a disadvantage.[17]

The divisiveness of religious segregation is another consequence of dual enrollment. "One of the great dangers of a shared time program," according to a government report "is the possible divisive effect of splitting the public school student body into groups identified with relgious denominations."[18] Under some dual enrollment procedures, parochial school pupils enter the public school as a group rather than as individuals, but the parochial school is their point of origin and loyalty. The entrance of a group during the regular class hours marks them as distinctive church units to the other pupils and particularly so if parochial students wear distinctive dress. "As President Duke of the College of Jewish Studies of Chicago has pointed out, some Jews would resent any plans, such as shared time, which would bring Catholics, Jews, or any other church-related student groups into the public schools as distinctive units."[19] The further effect of religious division in the school program is faced by the U.S. Office of Education. While generally favoring dual enrollment, it reports as one of the associated problems the fact that the participation of parochial school pupils "in public school extracurricular activities was restricted or curtailed because of scheduling problems or the policies of the participating schools."[20]

Since the genius of the American public school system lies in its nonsectarian emphasis, to identify teachers, pupils and administrators in terms of their faith through dual enrollment most certainly changes the sectarian irrelevance of the public school.

One of the most serious charges laid against dual enrollment is that it assumes such a close collaboration of public and parochial schools as greatly to increase religious and sectarian influence in public schools. Such collaboration is necessarily found in scheduling, grading and the choice of textbooks. The U.S. Office of Education survey reports a Michigan school superintendent as saying that, of necessity, an effective shared time program "will involve frequent meetings between the principals . . . involved, to clarify policy, philosophy, methods and procedures for attendance, marking, transfers of students, truancy, etc.," and "this close liaison should exist between counsellors and even faculty in so far as possible. . . ."[21]

Indeed, the same survey reveals that existing dual enrollment arrangements succeed only when there is joint planning and a "flexibility of administrative staffs in establishing new administrative procedures and operating patterns."[22]

This is a polite way of asserting the need for public school administrators to be open to parochial school desires. The same government survey reported that in Kearsley, Michigan, "the pastor of Holy Rosary expressed concern over the selection of public school textbooks for dually enrolled pupils, and as a result, nonpublic school teachers were invited to sit in on discussions of the selection of textbooks."[23] The survey also demonstrates that once liaison is established between public and parochial schools more than the dual enrollment program is discussed. In Kimberly, Wisconsin, for example, "contacts between the schools were informal and were concerned with educational matters of mutual concern, not limited to dual enrollment."[24]

One opponent of dual enrollment raises profound and disturbing questions concerning both the academic and administrative partnership between public and parochial schools implied in the program. He suggests that the public school teachers and administrators will

> be forced by the state to enter into a working relationship with the clergy and religious of the Roman Catholic Church, missioners who admittedly have one primary aim in life, the growth of their church and the propagation of its doctrinal viewpoint. What right has the state to compel public school personnel to enter into a liaison with the Roman Catholic or any other church in this fashion?[25]

There are administrative as well as academic consequences of dual enrollment. If dual enrollment becomes the accepted pattern it could not be confined only to public-parochial school participation, since no one should question the right of any group—left, right or center—to set up a school. A U.S. report notes that

> widespread establishment of shared time programs would weaken and ultimately destroy the nation's public school systems. If shared time arrangements are instituted, not only Catholic but also many Protestants and other religious and non-religious groups will want to participate in these programs. Will it be legally possible or democratically desirable to deny the same participating privilege to all religious and non-religious groups? Will it be permissible for legal and legitimate rightist and leftist organizations to teach history and social studies as part of the shared time programs? . . . [The] public school, one of the major contributions of our culture to civilization, will become a supplementary school, offering only that part of the educational program which parents and others consider relatively unimportant.[26]

However, even if such groups or the major Protestant churches do not organize parochial schools, the existing systems pose a serious administrative problem. In a given community where there is a Roman Catholic, a Lutheran, a Seventh Day Adventist school and a Christian Day School it is possible that each might want a different shared time arrangement with the public schools. "Scheduling of parochial and public school classes would be an almost impossible undertaking. What complex curriculum combinations can be arranged when each religious group decides how much or how little of the public school offering it wants and hundreds of children enter for some parts and few for other parts of the program?"[27] No public school can be expected to enter arrangements with all the special-interest groups in a community; yet an arrangement with only one or two implies a sectarian purpose as the reason for shared time.

It might be suggested that the average student in a university faces similar schedule problems if he wants to take courses offered by various departments or schools. These schedules are not, however, altered by or complicated by the pressure of parochial school administrators. The university is not obliged to rearrange its schedule to accommodate individual students, whereas a public school administrator would be expected to do so if this were necessary for the participation of an entire parochial school class.

Another Church–State problem that administrators must face is the location of public schools. This was illustrated by the U.S. Office of Education survey as follows:

> A *Kimberly* [*Wisconsin*] *public school official expressed concern that the location of a contemplated new junior high school building might be controlled by the dual enrollment program since participating schools would need to be relatively close. The contemplated new public school, he speculated, might be located near the nonpublic school instead of on a site best suited to the needs of the whole community or most economical to purchase.*[28]

Among other administrative problems listed in the U.S. Office of Education survey are the following: scheduling courses within a restricted time span; scheduling classes so that both dually enrolled and full-time pupils could be in the same classes; creating an appropriate assignment for full-time pupils and/or public-school teachers when the dually enrolled pupils were not in class because of differences in the calendars of the participating schools; noise created by the dually enrolled pupils as they entered or left the public schools as a group during the middle of the school day; shifts necessary in the instructional program in order to take into account the religious customs or the reduced number of hours available to instruct dually enrolled pupils who attended class on a slightly different schedule.

Other problems listed were: arranging for special after-school academic coaching for dually enrolled pupils who needed it but who attended afternoon classes at the nonpublic school; initial pupil adjustment to two different educational environments; arranging for nonresident tuition required by the public schools of pupils who did not reside in the public school district; coordinating schedules and arranging other administrative matters among the participating schools, especially when the nonpublic school pupils resided in several public school districts or there were several participating schools.

The disadvantages of dual school enrollment and the openness of a number of Roman Catholic educators suggest the value of experimenting with other approaches to religious education. In the new city of Columbia, Maryland, which is being built between Washington and Baltimore, an ecumenical approach in which plans are being made for reserved time is pivotal. Each day children are to be released for a given period to attend classes in religious education. In this new community there are to be no parochial schools.

In this context a creative suggestion was made by the Reverend John P. Cole, an educational officer in the Kansas City–St. Joseph Diocese. He proposed that Protestants yield on the traditional Sunday school approach by engaging in daily religious education, that Roman Catholics yield on parochial schools by abandoning general education and that public schools yield some part of each school day for religious education. "Churches might cooperate in establishing a religious education building adjacent to the public school campus." Churches would also supply the personnel for those students who wished to attend. Such religious teaching "would not be supported by the state or any tax funds." Father Cole also expressed an interest in the cooperation of Jewish and other religious groups.

In the foreseeable future it is quite likely that the problem of providing both religious and secular education will be explored on a number of levels. Some communities will continue to use released time, others will try dual enrollment or the objective teaching of religion or reserved time. In this transitional period it is important not to let the federal government or any other agency stampede the schools or the public into adopting one solution such as dual enrollment which presupposes one or more parochial school systems. In the long run such an approach is not likely to solve a problem facing those churches that do not operate parochial schools. The solution ought to lie ultimately in some cooperative ecumenical approach that will supplement and respect secular education rather than use it for the alleviation of a church school financial problem.

10

Elementary and Secondary Education Act of 1965

A new direction was given to education in the United States when Congress adopted the Elementary and Secondary Education Act of 1965 (ESEA). The goals of the act were help to educationally deprived children, improvement of library and textbook resources and stimulation of new and cooperative educational activity. ESEA was from the outset designed to provide concessions to parochial schools since earlier efforts to provide federal aid to public schools have been stalled in Congress by parochial school interests. A front-page story in the January 2, 1965, *New York Times* described the problem:

> *The decision to abandon the general-aid approach—stalled in Congress for a number of years because of the Church–State issue—was made after the President had sounded out a number of Representatives and Senators.*
>
> *The consensus, he discovered, was that a bill to provide general aid for teacher salaries and school construction limited to public schools would again be stalled by those advocating aid to parochial and private schools.*

The problem of reconciling the needs of the public schools with the demands of parochial school interests and the strictures of the establishment clause led the Administration and Congress to pass much of the Church–State problem to the local communities and thus minimize their own responsibility. The chief Church–State problems are in the first three of the six ESEA Titles. These can be summarized as follows:

TITLE I

Title I of ESEA provides for help to "educationally deprived children," but since there is some poverty in almost all school districts all but about 5 or 10 per cent of the school districts in the nation will receive some benefits. The Church–State problem arises from the requirement that public schools desirous of receiving public funds must offer public programs "to educationally deprived children enrolled in nonpublic schools without requiring those children to be in full-time attendance in the public school." [1] However, no specific program such as dual enrollment is mandatory. The act simply requires the local public school district to make "provision for including special educational services and arrangements (such as dual enrollment, educational radio and television and mobile educational services and equipment) in which such children can participate." [2]

In the event public funds are used to provide educational radio and television, only mobile equipment can be provided. Transmission lines would be precluded, whereas receiving sets would be permissible. Public educational agencies thus retain both ownership and administrative control over all property.

House Report 1814, which interprets the ESEA amendments of 1966, states:

Mobile equipment are tools of the public educational specialists providing remedial services to children and are not additions to the equipment of private schools. Any mobile equipment necessary for the conduct of such specialized service is to remain under the control of the public personnel. While it was and is intended that "mobile equipment" includes such equipment as movie projectors and portable television sets, their use off public school premises was and is prohibited except in providing "remedial services" as such term is amplified herein. It most certainly does not include any equipment which is, or is designed to be, affixed to the realty.[3]

TITLE II

Title II provides $100 million for fiscal year 1966 and additional funds for the following four years for "the acquisition of school library resources, textbooks, and other printed materials for the use of children and teachers in public and private elementary and secondary schools." Both the House and Senate Committee reports that interpret the bill use the following language:

The Committee has taken care to assure that funds provided under this title will not inure to the enrichment or benefit of any private institution by providing that:

(1) Library resources, textbooks, and other instructional material are to be made available to children and teachers and not to institutions;

(2) Such materials are made available on a loan basis only;

(3) Public authority must retain title and administrative control over such materials;

(4) Such materials must be those approved for use by public school authority in the State; and

(5) Books and materials must not supplant those being provided children but must supplement library resources, textbooks, and other instructional materials to assure that the legislation will furnish increased opportunities for learning. The State should also assure that the federal funds made available under this title will not be used to supplant or duplicate, inappropriately, functions of the public library system of the State.

Both committees also asserted that the operation of Title II "would not be different from the conduct of a public library program which makes available on a loan basis, library materials, unrestricted as to content, to both public and private school students."

The major Church–State issue in Title II revolves around the practice followed locally. If the library and textbook resources are in effect on permanent loan then they are to all practical purposes gifts rather than loans in the true library sense of that word.

Title III

This title provides for "supplementary education centers and services" with a first year authorization of $100 million. The supplementary services include guidance, counseling, remedial instruction, health and social work services, adult education, specialized instruction and equipment for handicapped or preschool children, radio and television programs and other special programs such as making available specially qualified personnel including artists and musicians on a temporary basis to public and other nonprofit schools and organizations.

The original bill of the Administration also provided for a partnership of public and parochial schools. It provided for supplementary educational centers and services, stating that "nonprofit private schools, public, and nonprofit private agencies" must participate "in the planning . . . and in the establishing and carrying out of that program. . . ." The Federal Commissioner of Education, Francis Keppel, spoke of this partnership philosophy in his Senate testimony when he said "centers will be administered by a partnership including the local educational agency." The partnership in effect would have given parochial school interests a practical veto over any program that did not please them. This partnership philosophy was rejected by congressional committees at the insistence of non-Catholic agencies, with the result that the law as enacted provides that the public school board "applying for a grant would have to involve persons broadly representative of the cultural and educational resources of the area to help plan and carry out the local program." Among these resources would be parochial schools.[4] Their concern would be represented, but under the legislation they would have no built-in veto.

If in practice parochial school interests seek to exercise a veto or promote a partnership philosophy, there would be a serious Church–State issue.

Title IV and Title V provide for research and development centers, support for research and measures to strengthen state educational agencies. Title VI includes a section intended to keep federal agencies from supervising or controlling the administration or curriculum or selection of library resources in local school systems. This section is largely meaningless since federal control is evident at other points in the act. For example, the act required local public schools to make certain arrangements with private schools if the public schools were to receive federal aid. Another provision in the law authorized the U.S. Commissioner of Education to make books and instructional materials available directly to parochial school pupils even in those states where it is forbidden by state constitutions. Quite clearly, should this feature of the act go unchallenged in the courts or be acknowledged as constitutional, it would render meaningless state constitutional provisions against aid to sectarian schools. Parochial school supporters could block state appropriations and local tax levies for public schools with the expectation that a more amenable federal government would provide its own program of educational services in which parochial schools would share.

ESEA was not completely satisfactory to either proponents or opponents of aid to parochial schools. It did, however, receive the support of Roman Catholic congressmen who had opposed general aid to public schools only, as embodied in a bill submitted by the Kennedy Administration to an earlier session of Congress. Representative James J. Delaney, one of the leaders in blocking legislation, was interviewed by an Associated Press reporter. "Is it fair to say you killed the Kennedy school bill?" he was asked. "Yes," he replied. "The bill was discriminatory from its inception. It would have helped only public schools. . . ." Delaney also answered yes to the question "Does the Johnson bill in general meet your objections to the Kennedy bill?"

Among other questions was one dealing with the bill's language, which left aid to parochial school pupils imprecise at some points. "Do you think the President should have been more explicit in saying how parochial schools are to benefit under his bill?" Delaney said, "No. I would prefer to see the language kept the way it is. The intent to aid all children is there. Anything more specific could exercise limitations. I would leave it to the Administration to carry out the intent of the law."[5] It is possible to infer from Delaney's answer that it would be easier to achieve broader aid through pressure on administrative agencies than would be possible from Congress. As we shall see later on, the U.S. Office of Education did subsequently write regulations that broadened the concept of aid to parochial schools.

A similar interpretation could be taken from an exchange during the House public hearings. Representative Hugh Carey (D., New York), who is known to speak for parochial school interests on the House Education Committee, noted that the bill opened the door for greater future aid to church schools:

> MR. CAREY: *"If I may suggest, the reference might well be made that Rome was not built in a day."*
> MSGR. McMANUS: *"I will take the allegory as you state it."*
> MR. CAREY: *"We have put a couple of good building blocks in this bill."*[6]

There were other proponents of aid to parochial schools who supported President Johnson's Elementary and Secondary Education Act even though it did not meet their expectations. Monsignor William McManus, superintendent of Roman Catholic Schools in Chicago, said:

> *The measure pending before this committee, let us face it, is not going to take any of the financial burden off the backs of benefactors and patrons of nonpublic schools. It will do no more than give some of the children, particularly the poorest of poor children attending them, an opportunity for an enriched education. . . . We must go along, even though the benefit to us is extremely limited, in the interest of taking care of these desperately poor children in both metropolitan and rural areas."*[7]

Those in the Roman Catholic Church who appeared in support of the bill were at the time moderates in light of the fact that Citizens for Educational Freedom, which takes an extreme position, was critical of any support for the bill. CEF wanted tuition grants for all children in parochial schools and not just aid for the disadvantaged.

Thus there are at least three different interpretations of ESEA by Roman Catholics concerned about parochial school education. One view is that it does not really aid parochial schools but had to be supported because it did aid the poor children in both public and parochial schools. A second view holds that the legislation should have been defeated because it didn't go far enough. The third position is that this legislation opens the door through administrative action and further legislation to more substantial aid for parochial schools.

Opponents of aid to parochial schools were similarly divided. Some Jewish, Protestant and civil libertarian groups opposed the Johnson bill because at certain points it provided public support for parochial schools. One of the provisions in the act on which opponents focused was dual school enrollment, or shared time. Opponents also objected to the use of public funds for providing personnel and equipment to parochial schools. The National Council of Churches, however, supported dual enrollment and other features of the bill on the assumption that children rather than parochial schools would benefit. The council accepted the "child benefit" theory with the understanding

1. *That benefits intended for all children be determined and administered directly by public agencies responsible to the electorate;*

2. *That such benefits intended for all children not be conveyed in such a way that religious institutions acquire property or the services of personnel thereby;*

3. *That such benefits intended for all children not be used directly or indirectly for the inculcation of religion or the teaching of sectarian doctrine; and*

4. *That there be no discrimination by race, religion, class, or national origin in the distribution of such benefits.*[8]

The continuing controversy over ESEA is a result of the administrative regulations prepared by the U.S. Office of Education after the bill was adopted, and of local practices and pressure from parochial school interests. The following examples will illustrate the origin and nature of the controversy:

One controversy between opponents and proponents of aid to parochial schools was presumably settled by an agreement in House debate and by the wording of the Senate Education Committee Report which clearly specified *that public school teachers will be made available to other than public school facilities only to provide specialized services which contribute particularly to meeting the special educational needs of educationally deprived children (such as therapeutic, remedial or welfare services). . . .*[9]

But when the Office of Education wrote the administrative regulations it approved many programs in parochial schools which Dean Kelley of the National Council of Churches asserts "are hard to recognize as even remotely 'therapeutic, remedial or welfare' in character—for instance, 'art, library and music education' in parochial schools in New York City."[10]

The administrative regulations, contrary to the intent of Congress, authorize "broadened instructional offerings—on nonprofit private school premises if such action is indicated to assure the success of the project or the effective participation by children enrolled in nonprofit private schools. . . ."[11]

Another regulation broadened the congressional phrase "mobile educational equipment" to include "portable" items. In New York City the word "portable" had made it possible for public schools to provide kitchen equipment and library shelves for parochial schools. "One can hardly conceive of *children* borrowing library shelves," wrote Dean Kelley; "surely that would be an aid to the institution more than to children."[12]

The Office of Education has also permitted the states to order library books and textbooks requested by the administrators of parochial schools. "A typical arrangement seems to be for each school, public or private, to receive a duplicate set of encyclopedias. Although stamped 'Public Property,' they are placed in the parochial school on 'indefinite loan'—which means they will never be seen again outside that school."[13]

States such as Maine, Montana, Arizona, Rhode Island and New Jersey

are simply dividing their allotments on a proportionate basis between public and private schools, the private schools' "share" being spent by the state agency for library resources requested by private school administrators, which are then shipped di-

rectly by the publishers to the private school where they become in effect, part of the private school library.[14]

This practice of providing textbook and library books for parochial schools out of public funds was challenged in a state court and appealed to the United States Supreme Court. Two boards of education each representing a school district in New York State brought an action against the state commissioner of education to prevent him from using public funds for the purchase of textbooks to be loaned to children in parochial schools.

The New York Supreme Court noted an earlier state court decision that the furnishing of school supplies to pupils "is at least indirectly in aid of the institution." In August, 1966, the court found the statute contrary to both the state and the federal constitutions. The provision of textbooks to private school pupils could, said the court, reach the point "where parents of students at private schools begin to rely upon the assistance of public moneys for textbooks and private schools anticipate this reliance in the preparation of their budgets." The court found this a violation of the establishment clause. It also said it was a violation of the free exercise clause in that if textbooks "become unacceptable" at some future time there would be "some form of financial compulsion present that would affect a purportedly voluntary decision by either a parent or a representative of a private school.[15]

On June 1, 1967, New York's highest court, the Court of Appeals, ruled in a 4–3 decision that the textbook loan law is constitutional in that state despite Article XI, Section 3, of the state constitution, which prohibited even indirect aid to sectarian schools.

The United States Supreme Court on June 10, 1968, in a 6–3 decision, held the textbook loan law constitutional since "no funds or books are furnished to parochial schools and the financial benefit is to parents and children, not to schools." The Court noted that the New York statute "does not authorize the loan of religious books," that "each book loaned must be approved by the public school authorities," and that "only secular books may receive approval."

Parochial school interests fed the controversy by seeking to expand the law and the regulations in order to get more aid for church schools. Such pressures were possible because ESEA was poorly drafted, without due regard for local Church–State conflicts and because ESEA at certain points implied partnership between public and parochial schools, which made public school administrators vulnerable to parochial school pressures. The partnership implications are evident in provisions for shared time, shared resources and mutual planning.

In New York City, for example, the public schools' "Superintendent Bernard E. Donovan, his professional staff, and the representatives of the nonpublic schools" were described in *The Catholic News* of April 28, 1966, as having "for nine months . . . worked regularly and cordially to hammer out meaningful programs." The same newspaper indicated that "services and equipment were shared; books and teachers were made available *to children where they were, . . .*" which means in parochial schools. After listing some of the services, the same story added: "Even music and art courses were permitted to parochial school children in their own schools and under federal and state guidelines." Shortly after the program began, the New York chapter of the American Jewish Committee protested the assignment of public school teachers to sectarian educational institutions.[16]

The position of the hierarchy in the New York area was made clear when the Brooklyn *Tablet* of April 21, 1966, printed the text of an address by Monsignor Eugene J. Molloy, superintendent of schools of the Brooklyn Diocese, to the National Catholic Education Association, the title of which was "The Partnership Between Public and Private Education." In this address, Monsignor Molloy made the point that public school services should be made available to children in parochial schools rather than expect the child to attend public school part-time, which is the share time or dual enrollment concept. "It should be clear to educators," he said, "that any service designed to assist a child educationally deprived will be more effective when provided in the school the child legally attends." A few days later, Monsignor George A. Kelly, secretary for education of the Archdiocese of New York, also asserted that "educators understood two things:

(1) it was better to bring services to the child; (2) services would be comparable for public and private school children." [17]

These statements by Monsignor Molloy and Monsignor Kelly reject the idea of shared time of children but ask both the shared time of public school teachers and public school resources.

Other pressures were brought to bear on Washington in an effort to get more aid for parochial schools in New York. "Father James A. Feeney, associate superintendent of schools for the Archdiocese of New York, said that a meeting was held in Washington Monday with officials of the U.S. Office of Education and the New York State Department of Education. As a result of this meeting Father Feeney said the Office of Education will send a task force to New York to work with city and state officials 'to review proposals and correct the unjust treatment of our children.'" [18]

About six months later the president of the 400,000-member United Parents Association of New York City told a state commission of the favoritism being shown to parochial schools. The October 11, 1966, *New York Times* reported:

> *Parochial schools, Mrs. Flast asserted, get one remedial reading teacher for every 100 retarded readers. The public school ratio, she said is "one for every 212 citywide" with none at all in some schools and only one in each special service school where there may be 500 to 1,000 children.*
>
> *Nonpublic schools, the parent spokesman said, get one remedial arithmetic teacher for every 100 retarded students with "no parallel in the public schools." Mrs. Flast added: "The same inequities pertain to the services of speech therapists, guidance counsellors, psychologists and social workers."*

Mrs. Flast also charged that there were "double standards for identifying poverty." Parochial schools were eligible for federal aid if 10 percent of their children were in the federal free-lunch program, whereas if such a criterion had been applied to public schools it would leave few public schools without such federal aid.

When the New York Board of Education seemed ready to yield to public protest by rectifying the inequities and by sticking more

closely to the intent of Congress, church pressures were intensified. Monsignor Raymond P. Rigney, superintendent of schools
for the Roman Catholic Archdiocese of New York and Monsignor
Molloy of Brooklyn threatened the New York board with a demand for a congressional investigation. Monsignor Rigney said
"it might be necessary to ask our representatives in Congress to
undertake a thorough study" of the way in which the City Board
spent last year's Title I funds as well as its plans for future funds.
Representative Hugh L. Carey (D.) of Brooklyn, who is the chief
parochial school spokesman in the U.S. House Subcommittee on
Education, joined in the threat. He indicated that it might "be
necessary for our Congressional delegation to undertake a series
of forums with city officials" if the Board of Education didn't
yield to parochial school demands.[19]

The pressures were also focused on the House Committee on
Education and Labor. That committee, which was initially responsive to complaints about Church–State abuses, inserted in
Part I of its supplementary report, issued August, 1966, language
designed to prevent or eliminate such abuses. Part II, however,
departed from the Church–State interpretation of the 1965 Act
by reinstating the partnership idea desired by parochial school
leaders. Part II of the supplementary report says:

> *The Committee will expect that the administration of Title I
> by the Office of Education will be pursued with strong require-
> ments to assure that there is meaningful and cooperative dis-
> course between public and private school administrators in
> devising projects in which the special educational needs of
> educationally deprived children who do not attend public school
> can be met.*[20]

The *Report from the Capital* of the Baptist Joint Committee on
Public Affairs indicated that "the new supplementary report on
the legislative intent of Congress opens many new and unspeci-
fied doors for regulations and guidelines from the Office of Education favoring parochial schools." The Baptist statement also
asserted that the House Committee report "serves notice that more
extensive attempts can be made in Congress to provide further
legislative aid to nonpublic education."[21]

It is significant, however, that the regulations issued by the Office of Education hewed closer to the requirements of Part I than might have been expected from the language of Part II, which had been designed to neutralize Part I.

This brief summary of ESEA abuses resulting from political pressure does not of course imply that the goals of the act or its implementation everywhere are to be disparaged. An American Civil Liberties Union pamphlet notes that ESEA "has in it enormous potential for strengthening educational opportunities for all Americans." But the ACLU pamphlet also issues this warning: "A combination of political pressure and poor drafting, however, have resulted in certain provisions which if not amended or administered strictly, may irrevocably damage the public school system and the principle of separation of Church and State."[22]

The Elementary and Secondary Education Act of 1965, whatever else may be said in criticism of it, did provide a pragmatic way to make available some greatly needed federal aid to education. In view of the history of earlier attempts to secure federal aid to education, some concessions to parochial schools seemed to be necessary for passage. These concessions were chiefly dual school enrollment, loans of mobile educational equipment, library resources and textbooks, and supplementary educational services. Of these, dual enrollment is far from acceptable to all proponents and all opponents of aid to parochial schools. Some advocates of aid prefer to use public school teachers in parochial schools rather than transfer children from one school to anotler. The precedent for transfer of selected teachers is included in ESEA as a supplementary educational service and thus opens the way for demands for more public school teachers for sectarian education. The indefinite loan of equipment and books to parochial schools by some local districts has to all practical purposes become a grant and thus aid to church schools in violation of the First Amendment. Genuine loans on the usual library basis and supplementary public education centers which all children and adults may use pose no Church–State problem and are among the finer features of ESEA.

11

The Dilemma of
Public Funds
for Church Colleges

At a recent legislative hearing, a state senator asked: "Why do you Protestants oppose government aid to parochial schools, while accepting it for your church colleges?" He was right in asking this question, because the inconsistency of Protestant practice needs to be explained. It would be easy to answer that Protestants oppose aid to parochial schools because they do not operate them, whereas they do have the expense of maintaining church colleges. Or one could say that this is an attempt to deny aid to Roman Catholic schools while getting it for Protestant colleges.

Neither of these is an adequate or accurate response. Practically all denominations accept government funds for their colleges and universities, whereas Protestant denominations that operate elementary and secondary schools—such as Lutherans, Adventists, Friends, Episcopalians—do not ask such aid for their weekday elementary and secondary schools. On the college level Protestant and Roman Catholic college administrators frequently collaborate in efforts to get government aid.

From a purely organizational perspective the inconsistency in practice can be explained by the fact that most Protestant colleges operate in complete or nearly complete independence of the official church. The college president and his board of trustees, rather than the church, are financially responsible for the college. Although many churches make supplemental grants to their institutions of higher learning, they rarely concern themselves with fiscal policy as such. When the issue arises, as it did in a Methodist Church–State study commission in 1963, there is often a clear division of opinion between those with church college responsibilities and those without them.

Many Protestant churchmen would argue that they are not inconsistent in their practice, because higher education presents a different problem from elementary and secondary education. They indicate that government grants to colleges and universities involve relatively few institutions in a few communities in contrast to the elementary and secondary schools that exist in practically every community in the nation. The Education Directory published by the U.S. Department of Education for 1966–67 lists 489 Protestant, 371 Roman Catholic, 11 interdenominational, 7 Jewish and 22 other church-related institutions of higher learning. Since a number of Protestant-related schools are related only nominally or traditionally, the actual number of church colleges is much smaller. If fewer than 800 church-related higher educational institutions (excluding theological seminaries) receive federal or state aid, public institutions are not affected to the degree that government aid to thousands of parochial schools would affect elementary and secondary public schools. The competition for the tax dollar is greater when there are large competing systems in each community.

Rightly or wrongly, many people believe that if public funds were available to parochial schools they would multiply by leaps and bounds. Today only about half the eligible Roman Catholic children attend parochial schools, but tax support might bring church pressure upon the rest to do so. And if the government supported elementary and secondary church schools, why shouldn't Protestants also seek such support? Colleges and universities are much more costly to launch and maintain so that not so much expansion in this area is likely to take place at the expense of public institutions.

Many Protestants do not feel that the denial of government aid to church elementary and secondary schools is discrimination against the Roman Catholic Church simply because Protestant colleges receive government funds. Roman Catholic colleges receive a commensurate share of public funds, as do private colleges that are unaffiliated. But if public funds were extended to church elementary and secondary schools, it would be aid chiefly to the one church that operates an extensive parochial school system.

Another reason frequently cited by those who wink at public support of church-related colleges is that there is no one pattern of religious affiliation on the college level as there is with parochial schools. Some church colleges are church-related only by tradition, do not have compulsory chapel or compulsory classes in religion and make no attempt to permeate the curriculum with religion as do parochial schools.

A few progressive churchmen add another perspective to the discussion. They note that many church colleges are racially and religiously integrated, whereas few parochial schools include pupils and teachers of other faiths. Most of them are still a haven for children whose parents do not want them to attend schools with Afro-Americans or others from minority groups. Government aid to colleges does not jeopardize racial desegregation as would similar aid to parochial schools.

The argument for government aid for nonpublic colleges is a pragmatic one since there are not enough colleges to accommodate all those who want higher education. Many legislators prefer to enlarge existing institutions of higher education rather than to construct a system of public colleges in communities throughout the state. This pragmatic argument does not apply to elementary and secondary education, since public schools exist in every community. These public schools are in a position to expand commensurate with the rate of population growth. There is no overweening educational need for parochial schools as such. If parents cannot or do not want to send their children to private elementary or secondary schools, the public schools are always open. This is not necessarily true with respect to state colleges or universities, which have limited dormitory and other facilities.

The distinctions cited above that tend to justify public aid to church colleges while denying such aid to church elementary and secondary schools are not acceptable to those who seek financial aid to parochial schools. In an article in the August 14, 1965, *America,* the Reverend Virgil Blum indicated that the case for government aid to parochial elementary and secondary schools is stronger than for colleges because of compulsory attendance laws. In response to this, Marvin M. Karpatkin, an American Civil Liberties Union attorney, wrote in the April 9, 1966, *America:*

> *Is it the compulsory feature of American public schools that is significant in this context? Or is it the fact that public schools are free? For those parents faced with the choice of sending children to a church school or a public school, does the compulsory clause have any relevance at all? In 20th century America there are few parents indeed who send their children to school only because the law requires it—and it would be hard to find any among those parents who are so strongly education-motivated that they send their children to private schools. Furthermore, the effect of compulsory attendence laws, applicable to church schools as well as public schools, is to discourage truancy and encourage attendance of church school children.*

Although it can be argued that the fact of aid to church colleges does not necessarily constitute a precedent for aid to church elementary and secondary schools, the problem of government aid to church colleges cannot be resolved solely on the basis of such differences. If the First Amendment denies government aid to churches for operating elementary and secondary schools, should it not also deny funds to church colleges and universities? An examination of the case generally advanced for public aid to church colleges reveals four major arguments:

1. One argument is that many church colleges are not owned or controlled by a church. Their relationship is merely traditional because church groups founded them or at one time controlled them. Therefore it would be an injustice to deny aid to colleges because of mere tradition. Such an argument does not justify aid to all church colleges but simply to those that to all practical purposes have so severed any meaningful church ties

as to be essentially secular educational institutions. The decision of whether a college is essentially sectarian or secular can in most instances be made by an examination of its catalogue.

The following are a few typical statements:

Fordham University, New York:

> The spirit and practice of Catholicism are strong and penetrating influences in the life of the Fordham undergraduate. They find deep and meaningful expression in theology courses required of all Catholic students, the organized retreats on and off campus, the opportunities for daily mass attendance, and finally the presence and availability of 200 Jesuit priests as spiritual guides and counsellors.[1]

Bellarmine College, Kentucky:

> As a Catholic college Bellarmine pursues its various objectives in harmony with Catholic doctrine concerning the purposes of life and education.[2]

Bethany College, Kansas:

> Bethany considers the Christian faith to be the unifying factor of all knowledge and believes its special educational mission to be the bringing of Christian insight to bear upon all human knowledge, philosophy and work.
>
> . . . the school was adopted by . . . the Augustana Lutheran Church one year after its inception and has been owned, controlled and generously supported by that body ever since.[3]

Friends University, Kansas:

> Friends University's Christian emphasis is grounded in the faith that only Christianity provides adequate solutions to the critical problems of our civilization. Such solutions are believed possible as a result of the experience of God in the living Christ which must be central to our college community.[4]

Assumption College, Massachusetts:

Assumption is a Catholic College. *Its entire curriculum is based on and derives its unity from the truths of Divine Revelation entrusted by Christ to His Church.*[5]

Creighton University, Nebraska:

Theology and sound cultivation of the Christian virtues will permeate the whole process.[6]

Morningside College, Iowa:

As a college related to the Methodist Church, Morningside seeks to lead her students to an understanding of Christian principles, especially as they are derived from the Bible. The college is committed to the Christian faith as an intellectual faith and as a vital way of life and conduct.[7]

Phillips University, Oklahoma:

The aim of Phillips University is to offer liberal courses of instruction in a vital Christian environment. . . . The Phillips faculty are Christian men and women. . . . While Phillips University is one of the Christian Church [Disciples of Christ] schools and the majority of its students come from this Brotherhood, there is no denominational test imposed. . . . Chapel service is scheduled at regular intervals and attendance is a requirement.[8]

The numerous colleges that carry similar statements of purpose serve a church interest as well as the interest of a group of parents who prefer to have a Christian education or atmosphere for their children. Precisely because they serve a church interest, they receive continuing church support. For the same reason they ought neither to expect nor to receive public subsidy via taxes. Some of them even make the point in their catalogues that they do not receive government funds. Perhaps this even strengthens their ability to appeal to private donors.

In June, 1966, the Maryland Court of Appeals ruled that state grants to three church colleges to help finance building construction violated the Establishment clause of the First Amendment to the United States Constitution.[9] Each of the colleges was examined to discover the stated purpose of the college, whether the college's governing board, officers, faculty and student body reflect any substantial religious control, the required participation of students in religious activities, and the place of religion in the college program. A fourth college was found to be loosely related to a church but without any requirement that any officer or faculty member be church related.[10] The court noted that the college's stated purposes in relation to religion are not of a fervent, intense, or passionate nature, but seem to be based largely upon its historical background."

In November, 1966, the United States Supreme Court permitted the Maryland decision to stand without further review. The decision remains binding for Maryland and because it was decided on federal grounds may be cited in courts of other states as well.

The Maryland case indicated that from the standpoint of the state, a merely nominal or traditional relationship to a church has no meaning if in fact the college is not, objectively speaking, a religious institution.

A more difficult problem is presented if church colleges try to maintain a nebulous position in order to claim they are church colleges when raising money from churches and nonsectarian when raising funds from the general community.

An article by a Roman Catholic educator pointed out that the Catholic college president is responsive to the kind of potential donors to whom he speaks:

> When the cardinal is on the dais and his listeners are Catholic, particularly potential alumni donors, he stresses the importance of Catholic higher education to the future of Catholicism in America. The accent is on the Catholic. When his audience is non-Catholic, particularly when it is composed of philanthropists and foundation executives, he stresses his institution's role in American higher education and its importance to the future of America. The role is hardly distinguishable from that of the secular campus across town. The accent is on education.[11]

This description easily fits the Protestant college president. Some Protestant church-related colleges with nothing but tradition to relate them to a church nevertheless find various ways to appeal to Protestant church bodies or to ministers as if they were performing a uniquely Methodist or Baptist role in higher education.

In fact, no college can at one and the same time be both a church college and nonsectarian. The problem is basically one of definition and such a definition is difficult. The following is an adaptation of the American Civil Liberties position. If an institution of higher education seeking government aid can subscribe to the following conditions it can be said to quality for aid as not being an establishment of religion.

a. No administrator, faculty member or student is required to be an adherent of any religious faith;

b. No administrator, student or faculty member is required to attend religious services or participate in religious programs of any kind or pass any religious test; nor be subject to disciplinary measures based on religious criteria;

c. The institution is not under the direction or control of any religious body or ecclesiastical officials;

d. It is not designed primarily to provide or promote religion or religious activity.

Those churches that maintain nominal relationships with colleges have never been so explicit in defining religion because they have been more concerned with institutional relationships than with religious realities. From the standpoint of the church and college, however, it is important to ask what is accomplished by calling a college "Christian" if it is not uniquely so? If the college does not serve distinctively religious purposes, its association with the church is at best nominal. Unless churches are beguiled into recruiting students or contributing support to such colleges, there can be no real advantage to the college in maintaining a fictitious church relationship.

2. A second argument for public aid to church colleges is, as Abraham A. Ribicoff, former Secretary of Health, Education and Welfare, once put it, that "the connection between religion and

education is less apparent and that religious indoctrination is less pervasive in a sectarian college curriculum" than in that of an elementary or secondary parochial school. This may be true in some colleges, but it is not true of all.

The issue, however, is not simply the degree of religious indoctrination relative to another type of institution but whether the institution that seeks a subsidy is in fact religiously oriented and/or controlled. A few nonsectarian colleges that have some religious emphasis but could meet the criteria proposed by the American Civil Liberties Union previously cited, would pose little problem. Where institutions of higher education are controlled by churches, there is generally some church benefit to be derived. In many Protestant colleges there are compulsory chapels or courses in religion. In Roman Catholic colleges and universities there are "crucifixes in the classrooms," the "Holy Ghost mass to inaugurate the academic year, spiritual retreats for the students and faculty" and other external evidence of religion.[12] Church doctrine is taught not only in undergraduate colleges but also in professional schools. For example, courses on legal and medical ethics are taught from a sectarian point of view in Roman Catholic schools of law and medicine, usually by a priest trained in moral theology.

Even such obvious external evidence does not tell the whole story. Wrote Edward Wakin:

> *Increasingly, Catholic educators look outside the classroom toward the campus community in order to establish a distinctively Catholic role in higher education. Talk has turned toward creation of a "vital" Catholic community of students and faculty characterized by commitment to the Catholic church and involvement in a vibrant life of corporate worship. Here at least it is felt that the campus can be Catholic.*

This in turn means that professors must be "alert, committed Catholics with a serious interest in theology."[13]

This description of Roman Catholic higher education has been paralleled for some time on a number of Protestant campuses except for two aspects. Much of this activity on Protestant campuses, while in a nominally Presbyterian or Methodist mold, for example, would be broadly Christian and few, if any, faculty members outside of the religion department would be expected to have "a serious interest in theology."

Roman Catholic campuses have a ratio of one priest for every thirty-five students, a ratio that no Protestant college would think of matching. Often, Protestant-related colleges have only a few ministers on an entire faculty. Nevertheless, Protestant colleges with more than a traditional church relationship are, like their Roman Catholic counterparts, religious institutions.

3. A third argument in support of public grants to church colleges is that there is a shortage of schools of higher education and an even greater shortage of public schools on this level. Therefore the government must support existing institutions to make them more able to serve the expanding population. In one sense this is a cogent argument. Yet the demands both of increasing population and for more advanced education make aid to church colleges at best a stop-gap solution. Many communities are rightly building junior colleges as well as four-year colleges. The federal government ought to use its aid to encourage municipal and state governments to provide more tuition-free public education.

4. A fourth argument is based on the distinction between the compulsory character of elementary and secondary education and the voluntary nature of higher education. Some spokesmen have advanced the idea that because students are mature enough to choose a nonreligious college or a religious college of their preference, aid to church colleges is not an infringement of their religious liberty.

The problem of course is not so simple. A student may live near a sectarian college and be forced by financial reasons to attend it so that he can live at home. Or he may want certain courses taught only at sectarian colleges in his part of the country. Or the absence of adequate housing or other facilities at nonsectarian colleges may force him into one he otherwise would not have chosen.

Actually, this is an irrelevant argument. The issue is not whether a student's religious liberty is violated but whether Congress has a right to aid church colleges. If it be argued that college attendance is not required, it can equally be argued that attendance at church services is not required in the United States. This, however, would not justify government aid to churches if they were in financial need.

Dr. John Bennett of Union Theological Seminary has presented another argument that parallels that used by Roman Catholic educators for aid to parochial schools. Bennett told the annual meeting of the Council of Protestant Colleges and Universities in 1963 that "if the state continues to aid the work of the private colleges but, because of the Church–State complications, the church-related colleges are excluded from such aid, the effect would be to punish church-related colleges." He went on to indicate that "This would be an intolerable kind of discrimination. This might, except in rare cases, cause church-related colleges to divest themselves of this relationship or make it almost impossible for most of them to compete with the aided private institution" [emphasis added].

Dr. Bennett, in charging discrimination, overlooks the fact that private secular colleges have no state or nationwide church membership to support them, no church officials to require or assess a percentage of contributions earmarked for colleges of that denomination. The private secular schools have to rely solely on alumni and other contributors unless they can obtain government support. So if the church college has everything the secular college has, plus the church support denied to the secular college, this is not discrimination but special privilege.

One possible conclusion to draw from the financial plight of church colleges is that the various denominations have expanded their higher educational systems beyond the ability of church members to support them. On the surface this does not seem to be the case since there are only 489 Protestant institutions of higher education. These are divided among 62 Protestant denominations. The largest listing is the Methodist, with 12 theological seminaries, 8 universities, 76 senior and 21 junior colleges. These are supported by ten million Methodists.

Another possible conclusion is that Protestant churches do not place a high enough priority on supporting colleges in their over-all church budgets.

The second point of Dr. Bennett's remarks is that Protestant church-related colleges would have to divest themselves of this relationship if they did not get state aid. This may be true of some colleges, but it is probably not true of the majority. Some church-related colleges have had more of a struggle than others, but there is no evidence that the alumni, the churches, the local businessmen or the foundations are prepared to stop supporting colleges that are worth supporting. The Denver *Post*, for example, announced on July 31, 1966, that "Denver area businessmen and their firms were a major factor in obtaining contributions and pledges of more than $1.5 million in the past year to help support academic, research and building programs at privately-financed University of Denver," a church-related institution.

Local businessmen support colleges, whether or not they are church-related, because they are private, contribute to community business and prestige and are also deductible recipients for income tax purposes.

Those colleges that cannot get adequate financing from their church or other private sources should give up their church relationship before they seek public funds. Educationally speaking, it was no disaster for Harvard or Yale or other one-time church colleges to have divested themselves of that relationship. It has not even prevented or damaged the existence of theological schools on their campuses. In terms of damage to the churches or to religion, there is little if any evidence to demonstrate that graduates of church colleges are ethically superior to graduates of secular institutions or that they are more devoted to their church.

A systematic study of the moral aspects of college life revealed that students at Notre Dame and Fordham were not greatly different from those at Columbia and Cornell. "A Jesuit sociologist, Robert McNamara, found the Catholic campus students restrained in sexual behavior (the reasons are social as well as religious), but relatively unrestrained in academic cheating."

The Greeley–Rossi study revealed on the basis of a nationwide survey that 93 per cent of those in Catholic colleges attended church weekly compared with 77 per cent of Roman Catholics on secular campuses, but 83 per cent of the Roman Catholic graduates of secular campuses were attending mass regularly one year after graduation. In comment on this Professor Wakin of Fordham adds:

While the differences in religious observance seem noteworthy, they cannot be automatically connected with the influence of the Catholic college. Catholic institutions attract more committed Catholics in the first place. Moreover, the significant finding by Father Greeley confirms the opinions of Catholic chaplains on secular campuses: non-Catholic campuses do not constitute a "serious peril" to the faith of "well-instructed" Catholics.[14]

Protestants and Roman Catholics alike should be increasingly aware that the overwhelming majority of students who are members of their churches are in secular colleges and universities. Much more could be done to help students and to foster an interest in the church if the church money now invested in church colleges were used to provide expanded staff and facilities for church centers on every secular campus in the nation. The average church college is a drain on the church's resources with too little to show for the investment compared with results from smaller investments in Wesley, Westminster and Newman foundations, Canterbury Clubs and the like. These church foundations do not exist at all secular universities, nor do they exist at many church campuses. The Methodist Church, for example, does not maintain Wesley Foundations at major Roman Catholic universities where both Protestant and nonchurch students attend. In order to maintain a college empire the churches put less than they should into secular campuses.

It can also be said as a result of personal investigation on many Protestant church-related campuses that at least as many students are alienated by church requirements or ethical rules as are helped by any official church relationship. Frequently the church as such gets the blame for compulsory chapel, compulsory courses in religion, reactionary social or academic attitudes and many other things for which the church as such may have no actual responsibility.

Church colleges are an asset to any denomination if they embody genuinely religious values in their atmosphere and faculty-student relationships. They should also offer courses that prepare students to be religiously sophisticated leaders in both church and society.

It is quite possible to be deeply concerned about both the values of church colleges and the values of government neutrality. Such a position might lead some churches to let some of their colleges become essentially nonsectarian private enterprises in order to channel their financial support into a few uniquely church schools. Top-flight church schools not only contribute to healthy pluralism in education but can set standards for secular state institutions to emulate. Today secular schools tend to set the standards for church colleges to follow because the churches do not adequately support their colleges and often do not insist on genuine freedom for faculty and students.

Thus far we have considered the arguments generally advanced for aiding church colleges while denying such aid to parochial schools, and the arguments for subsidizing church colleges on the same general basis as secular institutions. In the next chapter we shall examine specific types of government subsidy and their impact on church colleges.

12

Aid to Church Colleges

The American higher education problem is created by three phenomena. Population growth and the rising standard of living have increased the demand for college training. The National Industrial Conference Board estimates that about 9.5 million students will be enrolled in degree-granting institutions by 1975, a number almost triple the 1960 enrollment. Secondly, our technological society increasingly demands new skills as automation eliminates many unskilled and semiskilled jobs. It has been estimated that by 1970 the United States will be able to equal its 1960 output with 22 million fewer workers than it employed in 1960. Factory and service jobs are being eliminated at the rate of more than 17,000 a week. On the other hand, the U.S. Civil Rights Report for 1961 stated: "Even in a depressed area like Detroit, jobs were going begging for lack of skilled workers to fill them. It is estimated that for every 100 skilled workers the nation had in 1955 it will need 122 in 1965 and 145 in 1975." The only way most young Americans can get the added skills and knowledge is by higher education.

The third factor in the higher education problem is that, unlike our public school system, the colleges and universities of America are an outgrowth of a private school philosophy. Only those who can afford to attend may do so. Even the state colleges and universities often charge tuition, frequently discriminating against the children of lower income parents who simply cannot afford to enroll even in a state university. Of course American higher education was always discriminatory in terms of ability to pay, a problem sometimes softened by scholarships and campus job opportunities. But as the number of students increase and the necessity of employment skills also increase, private scholarships and campus job opportunities will not suffice to meet the individual costs of education, especially among economically depressed families.

A nation as rich as the United States can afford to provide public higher education for all who are able to do advanced work. Indeed, equality of educational opportunity ought to be extended to higher education. This means providing tuition-free public colleges in every sizable community in the nation. Direct or indirect subsidy of private, including church, colleges cannot possibly meet the need.

Just as throughout the United States there is a system of public elementary and secondary school education and a smaller parallel system of private and parochial schools, so pluralism is desirable on the higher education level. In practice that pluralism has already been obvious in those places where there are tuition-free or nearly tuition-free community colleges. But until there is a public community college available in every locality for those who want to attend, the United States cannot be said to have equality of opportunity in education. Government funds, with the exception of some legitimate research contracts, should be channeled into a public education system, the bulk of it going to tuition-free colleges.

For more than fifteen years, however, the federal government has pursued a makeshift policy of assisting existing secular and church colleges to expand in order to meet temporary needs. It has done so by means of loans for building construction, grants for fellowships or student loans, distribution of surplus real estate, research contracts and grants for library or other development purposes.

The College Housing Loan Program[1] that was adopted in 1950 authorized construction loans for new or improved housing and such other related items as dining rooms, student centers and infirmaries, for students and faculties. From the fiscal year 1951 through 1963, colleges and universities, including church colleges, received 1992 loans totaling $2.1 billion.

The argument for loans to church colleges is that government interest rates are well below the commercial rate and thus are an advantage to the borrower. This is also an argument against such loans since the difference between the government and commercial rate of interest is in effect federal aid to religious institutions.

The National Defense Student Loan Program,[2] which Congress included in the National Defense Education Act of 1958, authorized the granting of money to public and private nonprofit institutions of higher learning to make low interest loans to needy students. This act provided that for each year of teaching service in a public elementary or secondary school 10 per cent of a student's loan would be canceled, up to 50 per cent of the total. In 1964, amendments to the act extended the same cancellation of the loans to those teaching in private schools.

Since an overwhelming number of private schools are parochial, the net effect and undoubtedly the intent was to aid priests, nuns and lay teachers in church schools.

A similar program included in the same act authorized National Defense Fellowships.[3] Originally authorized were 1500 graduate study fellowships per year for periods not exceeding three years, but in 1964 the number was increased to 3000 for the 1965 fiscal year; 6000 for the 1966 fiscal year; and 7500 for each of the next two years. The fellowship includes a grant of $2000 to $2400 per year plus an allowance for dependents. Under the terms of the program, the cooperating institution is also subsidized by a direct federal payment not to exceed $2500 per person receiving a fellowship. During the first three years of this program the payments to institutions, including those that are church-related, totalled $18,061,000.[4]

A series of federal government grants or contracts have also been authorized by the National Defense Education Act of 1958. These include contracts to operate institutes for advanced study in counseling and guidance training, to establish and operate modern language and area study centers, to operate institutes for advanced study in teaching or supervising teachers of certain studies, and in training library personnel for elementary and secondary schools.

The Higher Education Facilities Act of 1963 authorized both direct and indirect funds for colleges and universities. Title II provided for grants up to 33⅓ per cent of construction projects to establish or improve existing graduate schools.[5] Of the first twenty-three such grants two were to church institutions, both Roman Catholic: $1,253,000 to Georgetown University, Washington, D.C.; and $112,123 to Our Lady of the Lake College, San Antonio, Texas.[6] Title III of the same act authorized loans for a fifty-year period for construction of academic facilities other than for sectarian instruction or religious worship. The loans were at interest rates well below the commercial rate and thus constituted an advantage to the borrowers. They were available for church institutions as well as others.[7]

A number of church institutions have been given substantial aid in the form of surplus real estate and personal property as a result of the Federal Property and Administrative Services Act of 1949.[8] The surplus real estate is made available for educational and public health purposes at a so-called public benefit discount, which can be as much as 100 per cent of the appraised fair value. This surplus property program is available to church institutions as well as others and is not limited to institutions of higher education but is available for elementary and secondary schools and hospitals.

The Elementary and Secondary Education Act of 1965[9] authorizes grants to colleges and universities for training and research in education but not for training in sectarian instruction. It also authorizes grants for construction and operating costs of facilities for research and related purposes. In each case, church institutions as well as others may benefit, although theological schools are specifically barred from grants.

The program of government scholarships and fellowships is not uniform. In some cases grants are made directly to the student, whereas in others they are made to the institution to give to students. In still others the college or university receives a matching stipend. In contrast to present practice, a policy of government neutrality in religion would result in the awarding of scholarships or fellowships on the basis of academic ability or as a result of public competition or individual application after public announcement. The institution where a scholarship or fellowship is used should be of no concern to the government if it meets the standards for such study. There would thus be no problem if such grants were in fact used in church colleges.

The awarding of public funds directly to church colleges for distribution or as matching grants does constitute a subsidy of religious institutions. The effect of such grants to students via church colleges is to give the college a means of encouraging individuals to enroll in the institution offering the scholarship. In 1963–64, private colleges and universities, including those with church affiliations, received 30.4 per cent of their total income from tuition and fees, 5.7 per cent from endowment earnings, 10.6 per cent from private gifts and grants, and 6.0 per cent from other educational and general income. State and local government provided only 1.3 per cent, whereas federal government provided 24.8 per cent through research grants and 1.7 per cent in other income. Since church as well as secular private colleges must meet their operating expenses from various sources, any government program providing church colleges with tuition scholarships or per capita grants on the basis of the number enrolled would be an obvious subsidy of the church institution as such.

At the state level, some church interests have encouraged legislation providing for tuition grants to students enrolled in church colleges. Such a measure was adopted in Michigan in 1966. This is part of a strategy planned by Citizens for Educational Freedom, to set a precedent for the idea that the "public tax education dollar belongs to the student and not to a school district. And further that the student has the freedom to spend that tax education dollar where he wants to spend it, either in a public or parochial school." [10] In consequence a C.E.F. sponsored bill was introduced in the Michigan legislature in February 1968 providing for tuition grants to children in parochial schools.

The Higher Education Act of 1965 authorized grants of $50 million a year through fiscal year 1968 for library assistance to private colleges and universities, $50 million for the same years to strengthen community service programs, and $55 million for 1966 to assist in raising the academic quality of colleges "which because of a lack of finances (and for other reasons) are struggling to survive and are isolated from the main currents of academic life." Congress also authorized $70 million a year through 1968 for payments to institutions in the form of educational opportunity grants to high school graduates who need aid to attend college. In the same act, Congress included authority to appropriate $129 million for fiscal year 1966, $165 million for fiscal year 1967 and $200 million for fiscal year 1968 to carry out college work-study programs and promote part-time employment of students, particularly those from low-income families. Another provision of the act established a National Teacher Corps for children in low-income areas and provided fellowships for teachers.

A major form of federal government subsidies of institutions of higher learning is the research grant. Research programs are administered by the Department of Defense, Atomic Energy Commission, National Science Foundation, the National Aeronautics and Space Administration, Department of Health, Education and Welfare and other agencies. In 1962 about $613 million was spent for research in colleges and universities. Ninety per cent of this went to 100 institutions, 59 per cent of which went to 25 schools. The first 25 did not include any church-related schools, but the following universities were among the next 75 institutions in the approximate order of the size of their expenditures: Yeshiva (Jewish); Baylor (Baptist); Denver (Methodist); Georgetown (Roman Catholic); Emory (Methodist); Marquette (Roman Catholic); St. Louis (Roman Catholic); Notre Dame (Roman Catholic).[11]

In 1966 the Department of Defense list of the 50 top military research contractors among universities included University of Denver (Methodist) $5,074,000; University of Dayton (Roman Catholic) $3,670,000; Duke University (Methodist) $2,631,000; American University (Methodist) $2,594,000; Syracuse University (Methodist) $1,119,000.

There are a number of reasons for government research contracts with church-related schools. One is that the government is merely purchasing a service and thus gets its money's worth in return. Another is that a strong, well-financed research program attracts strong faculty members. In turn this strengthens the intellectual and cultural life of the church-related school. Some even suggest that a church's Christian responsibility for the nation creates a moral obligation to accept government contracts.

On the other hand, there are some important reasons for excluding church colleges from government research contracts. One of these is that the basic responsibility of the church college is uniquely to serve the church in its religious calling. Insofar as a church college depends or comes to depend on government contracts to pay for any of its faculties it becomes dependent on public funds and risks losing or compromising its special religious position. It does so in at least two ways: A church-related college can feel that there is a greater financial and prestige potential from maximizing its government relationship and minimizing its church connection. If so it compromises its uniqueness as a religious institution by subtly changing the educational orientation which was intended by the church that founded and supported it. Secondly, the church college or university compromises its religious position by accepting research contracts that support military purposes. Aside from the obvious moral problems involved when a church institution performs military research, the nature of the church's ecumenical relations and missionary efforts can be irreparably damaged. The missionary work or ecumenical program of the Christian church with Buddhists or Christians in Vietnam would be shattered were they to learn that some of the weapons used against them had been created or perfected by research done in a church-supported university under contract to the Defense Department.

The bulk of all research in colleges and universities is paid for by some branch of the armed forces or a related agency such as the Atomic Energy Commission. Such government agencies also ask for research in fields that may sooner or later bear fruit in military ways. Often government research projects require by contract specification that the results and methods of such research be kept secret and the personnel involved be screened. Such investigation of personnel and secrecy is contrary to the best traditions of academic freedom and the free flow and discussion of information that characterize a good university.

Finally, government research contracts with church colleges support the academic programs and personnel of church institutions. Some of these institutions choose faculty and administration on a sectarian basis with the result that the sectarian purposes of the school are directly served.

There is some evidence that military agencies have tried to control their university research projects.[12] But there is no evidence of government as such trying to control an entire university. The problem of control is more subtle. Certain universities, for example, get substantial federal research contracts because of the capabilities of their faculty or equipment and the cooperative attitude of university personnel. If another institution, desirous of getting a research contract or a larger share of available research dollars, were to change its faculty or structure in order to be more attractive for government research activity, a type of control would have been imposed on it.

It is possible in theory to assert that government research contracts with church institutions, designed to produce needed information for the public health, safety and welfare, do not pose Church–State problems, provided the contracts are genuine business arrangements concerning a specific service to be performed in a specific period of time. Such contracts, however, should not be intended as an indirect subsidy of the university or result in capital improvements, which the university retains. The U.S. Department of Health, Education and Welfare pays a flat 15 per cent overhead on these contracts. The armed forces, however, subsidize the universities as such by providing management allowances or overhead costs that may involve as much as 50 to 70 per cent of its research contract.[13]

Although no clear-cut constitutional violation of separation of Church and State may be involved in genuine research contracts, the Church may well question the use of a church college's science department for extensive government work. This is not only because it may divert faculties from teaching but also because the nature of much of government research may be completely alien to the peaceful creative purposes that motivate the church.

In the final analysis the United States has a Church–State problem in higher education because there has never been adequate planning at any governmental level to take care of the increasing need for education beyond the high school level. Efforts by government and college officials have almost without exception been aimed at temporary palliatives such as the expansion of existing facilities. These include grants for new buildings. The June 18, 1965, *New York Times* reported that St. Francis College in Brooklyn announced receipt of a federal grant of $1,115,916 to build a $3.5 million science center. "The Rev. Urban Gonnoud, president of the college, said the new building would enable the college to increase the full-time enrollment from the present 1,200 to 2,000 students." This expansion barely scratches the surface of the need, but it is evidence of aid to the general church program even though it is a gift for what purports to be a nonsectarian science building.

Another palliative is the tax credit proposal advanced in 1965 in the U.S. Senate by Senators Peter Dominick and Abraham Ribicoff and cosponsored by thirty-three other senators. They sought provision of a yearly maximum of $325 in federal income tax credit for the first $1500 paid for tuition, fees, books and supplies for each student "at an approved college or university." [14] Such a proposal would solve nothing, for it would give colleges an excuse to raise tuition fees by approximately the amount of the tax credit; short of that it would aid only those families in middle- and upper-income brackets.

If with federal assistance state and local governments were to provide adequately for secular higher education, there would be no public need to subsidize church colleges. The churches that own or otherwise maintain a relationship with institutions of higher education would then have to choose adequately to support a few uniquely religious colleges or to encourage them to become secular in order to receive government support. Such an approach to the Church–State problem need not result in the elimination of most church colleges. Rather, it would cause a reexamination of the role of the church in higher education, hopefully leading both to a distinctively Jewish and Christian contribution to learning and to more adequate church funding of student religious activities at or near each secular campus.

13

An Exceptional Case: The Amish

In November, 1966, the Supreme Court of Kansas upheld the arrest and conviction of Leroy Garber, a forty-one-year-old Hutchinson, Kansas, Amishman, for failure to have his daughter "attend continuously a public school or a private, denominational or parochial school taught by a competent instructor" as the Kansas law provided.[1] Sharon Garber had attended and completed her eighth-grade work at a rural public elementary school whose classes were largely composed of Amish children but had not entered the public high school.

In 1965 the Kansas compulsory school attendance law had been amended to require attendance to the age of sixteen. It was amended also to eliminate the provision that the law should not apply to any child who had completed the eighth grade. In effect the law required Leroy Garber to send his daughter to the public high school or an equivalent private school. Garber and the other Amish, however, oppose sending their children to "worldly" schools such as a large consolidated school where their children would be taught by non-Amish teachers and where the dominant culture of their teen-age classmates would be quite different from that of the Amish.

The Old Order Amish, who are descended from Swiss Anabaptists, follow the ethic of the early Christian church which includes nonresistance and sharing of material aid. In addition they are rural folk who believe in living close to the soil, dress plainly and oppose automobiles, electricity, telephones and higher education. They operate parochial schools for essentially two reasons: to combine religion and education and to keep their children from the worldly influences that would destroy their way of life.

The Amish are law-abiding. There is no known case of one of their members being imprisoned for a felony. Rather than flout the law, Garber tried to comply by enrolling his daughter in two schools. One was the Amish Harmony vocational school established following the amendment of the school law by a group of Amish in Yoder, Kansas. The school was limited to those who had completed the eighth grade but had not yet reached sixteen years of age. In addition, Sharon Garber was enrolled as a high school student in the American School, a correspondence school in Chicago which is approved by the United States Office of Education.

The Amish Harmony school was taught by an Amish farmer one morning each week. In addition, students were required to study an hour a day at home and spend five additional hours a day on assigned vocational projects in home and farm management, following which written reports were submitted to the instructor. Standard textbooks were used for study of English, American Government and Kansas history. The teaching was in English, but the students also studied German. The instructor, however, had had only an eighth-grade education.

The Kansas Supreme Court held that the American and the Harmony schools were "essentially home instruction systems" and hence did not fit within current Kansas law. The Kansas legislature in 1903 had eliminated a provision for home instruction which had required the "same examination as other pupils of the district or city in which the child resides. . . ."[2] The Kansas court noted that the legislature had made "no provision for such equivalent instruction as the basis for exemption. However, in its discussion of religious liberty, the court affirmed the right of parents "to educate their children elsewhere than in the public schools provided the state's minimum educational requirements are met." By minimum educational requirements the court and legislature meant continuous attendance at public, private or parochial schools. The court also "distinguished between religious beliefs and religious practices," holding that the First Amendment protected the former but not necessarily the latter.

The issue in the Garber case is one of religious liberty—whether the state can prescribe certain types of schools that everyone without exception must attend, or whether educational requirements can be met in other ways.

The argument against the Amish position is that the state has a responsibility to children to equip them to be citizens in the total society. The Amish parents on the other hand want to equip them only for life in an Amish rural community. If all other citizens are expected to send their children to public, private or church schools that meet certain state requirements, why should an exception be granted to the Amish? Would this not lead to a complete release of all churches from civil and secular authority, thus making churches a law unto themselves?

The argument for the Amish position is that the state rightly prescribes certain educational standards but not the precise way in which those standards are to be met. For example, a state may require a minimum knowledge of such subjects as arithmetic, English, history and the like but need not prescribe the specific textbook or the manner in which the subjects are taught. This would mean that a child who could by standard examination meet the minimum legal requirements could be considered to have a required minimum education.

The United States Supreme Court has acknowledged the right of private and parochial schools to operate, in effect providing for freedom of choice, including schools based on religion. Should not other types of education be similarly recognized, including tutorial and correspondence courses, when religious conviction would be violated by attendance at public schools? The fact of parochial schools does not always mean a parallel school system in terms of teacher qualification or comparable equipment. For example, more than forty states of the Union, including Kansas, do not require private or parochial schools to employ certified teachers. A booklet of the National Committee for Amish Religious Freedom adds that "there is no data to prove that there is any connection between state standards and pupil learning." The same booklet also indicated that "those states which have tested Amish students are satisfied with accomplishments of the Amish teachers. . . ."[3]

A second consideration in stating the case for the Amish is that proposed in another context by Roger Baldwin, former executive director of the American Civil Liberties Union. He said: "I think that in general the A.C.L.U. should put conscience in a preferred category over law when no social damage results to others."

There is no evidence that honoring the conscience of some fifty thousand Amishmen would do social damage in any state or interfere with the public order. In fact it could be argued that the protection of nonconformist groups whose unique culture adds to the quality of our national life is a contribution to liberty, which in the United States is so much a part of the public order. Professor Philip B. Kurland of the University of Chicago Law School indicates that "the smaller the religious group, the greater the requirement that the state accommodate to its needs."[4]

Some have suggested that a provision for conscientious objection for a few could injure the public order if extended to hundreds of thousands of American instead of simply to a few. Actually there is very little danger of this. The major groups that seek withdrawal from public schools by operating parochial schools are not interested in a general withdrawal from secular political and social life, as are the Amish. Rather, they want their children to be able to compete with others in the economic, intellectual and political life of the nation.

Yet it should also be noted that if any substantial number of citizens, such as 500,000 to a million, were to refuse on grounds of conscience to comply with a specific school law, many citizens would still prefer to make some provision for them rather than have them flee the country, as some Amish have already done.

The Kansas Supreme Court was right in asserting that the rights of parents are not absolute and may be restricted by law to guard the welfare of children. But by the same token the right of the state is not absolute. The state has the right, for example, to set minimum educational standards, but these need not be so restrictive as to exclude some forms of education that can prepare youth to pass state examinations. The National Board of the American Civil Liberties Union made the following appropriate statement in 1966: "The consciences of such parents should not be overridden unless the state demonstrates that its requirement is essential to the preservation of the safety, health or welfare of the children. Amish education appears not to have been detrimental to the children. . . ."

One solution to the Amish school problem was worked out in Iowa to the satisfaction of both the Amish and state officials. Following a crisis in 1965 when Amish children fled into the cornfields rather than be rounded up to attend schools with certified teachers, and Amish fathers went to jail and their property was confiscated, Governor Harold Hughes appointed a special study committee. The committee report acknowledged that Iowa could tolerate reasonable dissent from state laws provided certain minimum standards are maintained. The committee proposed a bill, which the legislature adopted. This bill provided that exemption from state standards would be granted by the state superintendent of public instruction, with approval of the State Board of Public Instruction, to Amish schools that apply for such exemption.

After an initial two-year exemption there must be yearly application by the school for renewal. Renewal may be conditional upon the students in these schools, who must demonstrate through examinations their knowledge of basic subjects. One state representative "said the tests called for in the bill will gradually bring the Amish a higher level of education than they now have. . . ."[5]

Actually the first tests of Amish pupils found them deficient in the technological knowledge required by modern society but objectionable to the Amish, who do not want to be a part of our modern technological society. There is thus a clear difference of conviction that may cause further problems. Apparently the legislation did not preclude the use of tests that would nullify the purpose of the legislation.

The legislation, which would affect schools attended by perhaps five hundred of the fifteen hundred Amish children of school age in Iowa, has at least one unfortunate provision. It is limited to members of religious organizations established for ten years or more and thus is discriminatory against more recently organized groups.

In considering the issue posed by the Amish it is important to ask whether the state does have an obligation to provide each child with an education for participation in every aspect of society. One answer is that the state makes no such claim. City youth are not prepared in the public schools for participation in farm life but for the culture in which they are being reared. Why should Amish youth be expected to prepare for a culture alien to their surroundings and background?

It can also be said that the state's obligation in the area of education is to prepare its youth for participation in the economic and political life of a democracy, with the respect for differing opinions which this implies. The graduates of Amish schools are literate enough to participate if they so desire in community decision-making. They are also so successful economically that there is no record of an Amishman on public welfare since the sect settled in Colonial America.

One further argument against the Amish position was mentioned by the Kansas Supreme Court. The court held that "religious liberty includes the absolute right to believe but only a limited right to act." In support of this the court cited *Reynolds vs. U.S.*, which held that a Morman had no right to practice polygamy even though he believed plural marriages were divinely ordained.[6]

In comment on this the National Committee for Amish Religious Freedom said:

> *The court did not consider whether there might be a difference between the constitutional power of the state to prohibit practices condemned by society generally . . . (as in the polygamy case), and the power to force a person to engage in activities that his religion condemns. The state surely has such power in some situations, where vital social interests or the rights of other persons would otherwise be immediately threatened. But the avoidance of standard education by the Amish poses no such threat.*

The U.S. Supreme Court, for example, in *West Virginia Board of Education vs. Barnette,* held that the freedom-of-religion clause permitted Jehovah's Witnesses to instruct their children not to engage in the flag salute.[7]

Clearly the issue raised by the Amish is exceptional and will not greatly affect the over-all problem facing public or parochial education in the United States. Yet no one concerned about the values of religious liberty implicit in the First Amendment can ignore such an issue of conscience as the Amish raise. Congress exempted from compulsory Social Security taxation those who, like the Amish, object to such taxation for religious reasons and who make no claims for Social Security benefits. Such exemption and the right of conscience granted by Congress to religious objectors to war can surely be extended to those who object to certain methods of fulfilling the educational requirements of the state.

14

Catholic Action
Since the Vatican Council

The high hopes of many Protestants and Jews that the Vatican Council would change church doctrine in the crucial area of Church–State and education have not been fulfilled. Here and there a few bishops and priests have demonstrated a willingness to find new approaches to education that would make cooperation with all religious groups possible. But on the whole the political demands of the hierarchy for public funds have been greater and more insistent than before the Vatican Council convened.

This fact of new political demands for public aid to church schools is probably the biggest single factor causing and perpetuating suspicion and hostility in an otherwise ecumenical era of friendly dialogue. This writer has heard Protestant laymen question whether any change with respect to religious liberty has actually taken place in Roman Catholic doctrine. In one way or another they have indicated that "actions speak louder than words." Likewise, Catholic laymen who sincerely believe they are entitled to tax relief are resentful of Protestant questioning of such claims. The Reverend John P. Cole alluded to this problem in the January 20, 1967, *Catholic Reporter*. He wrote:

I find it easy to kneel or stand and pray to the Father with one of my Protestant friends, either lay or clerical. But I find, almost invariably, that when we begin to talk about schools, public and private, we are a thousand miles apart. . . . The unity we begin to enjoy in prayer is shattered and we walk away from one another still separated, maybe even more so.

How shall we explain the combination of a new irenic attitude toward non-Roman Catholics that is the product of the Second Vatican Council, and the continued aggressive effort by Catholic leaders to get state subsidies for parochial schools?

The answer that there is already too great an investment in their schools or that the maintenance and expansion of this investment is proving too costly is inadequate, even though true. The deeper reasons are partly financial, partly emotional and partly rooted in tradition. Certainly one reason is a conviction that they are entitled to receive for their church schools their share of taxes. Most Americans, however, do not operate on the assumption that they are entitled to ask benefits for specific private institutions from the taxes they pay or that they are entitled to draw on public funds to pay for their participation in private organizations. Therefore, what many Roman Catholics think is due them as a matter of justice others see as a type of special pleading.

Perhaps it is impossible to understand the activity of Roman Catholics seeking government aid without noting that their determination to get adequate financing for their schools is the result of their attachment to parochial education. This attachment is rooted in a natural desire to have their children educated in a certain religious atmosphere. Yet for many Roman Catholics there are certain fears that also contribute to their commitment to parochial schools.

The first of these fears is that of "indifferentism," the idea or belief that one religion is as good as another. Although few if any Protestant theologians would make a case for "indifferentism," there is a sense in which the American spirit fosters the idea that it doesn't matter to which church you belong so long as you are "religious."

This fear of "indifferentism" is the basic reason for inserting in the Declaration of Religious Liberty of the Vatican Council the statement, which did not belong there, that "this one true religion subsists in the Catholic and Apostolic Church. . . ." It is this reason that impels Roman Catholics to expand their parochial schools in a day when they are no longer in a "state of siege" and when real or imagined Protestant hostility is changing to friendliness.

The second fear is secularism. The traditional Roman Catholic model of society is one dominated by the Church. In spite of the Vatican Council's Declarations on Religious Liberty and on the Church and the World, the Church has not yet come to terms with the secular world. It does not see that a powerless church in the spirit of her Master can have more real influence in society than a church that consciously seeks power. Or, put another way, there is a continuing desire to see sacred symbols and ceremonies, Catholic schools and hospitals, and so on, scattered throughout society in an effort to create a nominally Catholic or Christian culture in contrast to a reliance on the leaven of loving members at work in the secular world. It seems far more important, for example, to have children in Catholic elementary, secondary and higher education than bearing their witness in a secular public or private school.

Most Roman Catholics of course would not make this contrast, for they would assert the importance of both emphases. Yet in practice the concentration on public display of unique symbols and the building of "set apart" institutions does contribute to the loss of meaning of the symbols and to the insulation of those who work, teach or study in "set apart" institutions. This problem is not alone a Roman Catholic problem but a Christian one, as was suggested in Chapter 4.

Still another way of describing the same problem is to call it cultural or political Catholicism. The cultural or political Catholic fears a secular society or state because it is independent of the Roman Catholic Church, rather than because its values are pagan. The fear of a secular society that has accepted many Christian values is for some church leaders just as great as the fear of one that is wholly pagan.

Political or cultural Catholicism is content if it can link, integrate or unify the secular with Christian symbols and if it can get secular acceptance and support of Catholic education or other Catholic programs. It tends to emphasize Christianizing or Catholicizing rather than the evangelizing of society. Society can be baptized into the Church without becoming "just" or "loving," if only it accords a suitable role to church symbols, institutions, ceremonies and hierarchy.

The third fear is communism. Rabbi Arthur Hertzberg summarized this fear in an article in the December, 1962, *Commentary*. After stating that "Catholics have largely replaced Protestants as the guardians of that whole complex of practices once created to serve a sub-Protestant public piety," he listed the fear of communism as one of the reasons for this policy:

Christianity as a whole has lost heavily in recent decades and the Catholic Church more heavily than Protestantism. Naturally, the danger from communism is most immediate to the heaviest losers. To the Catholic mind, schooled as it is to think in terms of faith and dogma, the confrontation with communism is a war of ideas between religion and anti-religion. America, as the leader of the West, is cast for the role of the knightly defender of the faith. But for America to be true to this sacred mission, the Christian character of her public life must be buttressed. Parochial schools will teach the Catholics; and the children of others must get at least enough indoctrination in the public schools to give them an appreciation of the trust which as Americans they bear.

The assumption that religious indoctrination prevents communism is belied however by the fact of communism in heavily Roman Catholic and Eastern Orthodox lands in Eastern Europe, and by the large Communist voting bloc in Italy where Roman Catholic priests teach religion in the public schools.

Moreover, the identification of religious faith with or against any partisan political position perverts religion and creates antagonism on the part of opposing political groups. Many Europeans and Asians who are as opposed to communism as are most Americans believe it must be opposed on a political and economic level. They seriously question the identification of the church with a nation or any political group to such a degree that either the ideology of political allies or opposition to the ideology of political enemies becomes an article of faith.

Rabbi Hertzberg puts it in more American terms:

> The faith-counterfaith definition of the West's struggle with communism in fact contains the seed of America's certain defeat in the world at large. For what America can uniquely offer to the peoples of Asia and Africa is not the vision of a Christian or a Judeo-Christian society but precisely of a pluralistic world order in which all men are permitted, nay, encouraged, to pursue their own faiths, hopes and aspirations.[1]

These fears are not the only motivation for parochial schools, but they may be more understandable to Protestants than the desire of some Roman Catholics to receive a share of their taxes for their church schools.

Yet the Roman Catholic Church is certainly not the only religious group that seeks or accepts government aid for church institutions. Protestant college and hospital administrators, for example, also take advantage of every opportunity for public aid for their institutions. Whereas Roman Catholics are simply following their traditional theory of Church–State relations, Protestant college and hospital administrators have betrayed the Protestant tradition that opposes state subsidy of church institutions. The chief difference in approach to this question of state aid is that no Protestant denomination, separately or together with others, plans and launches a membership-wide political campaign for government aid to its own institutions.

The basic reason for this difference in approach lies in the differing conceptions of the Church. A church in the tradition of establishment tends to look upon all of society as related to the one true church with an obligation to support it. This is a quite different approach from those churches that have broken with the establishment idea. They expect financial and other support only from their own members and sympathizers. They have an obligation to improve society but do not expect society to support them in their improvement program.

A by-product of the identification of the welfare of the institution with the welfare of society is the willingness to see other social programs suffer if the institutional purpose is not served. This was nowhere more apparent than in the campaign during 1961 to get Congress to approve federal aid to education. The March 3, 1961, *New York Times* reported that "the hierarchy of the Roman Catholic Church in the United States has decided to oppose any school aid legislation that fails to help children attending private schools."

That campaign during 1961 preceded the Second Vatican Council. Since a wholly new spirit has emerged from that Council, only post-Council events should be considered.

Any objective survey of political activity by parochial school proponents since the Vatican Council, however, provides evidence that the Roman Catholic hierarchy's concept of religious liberty is by and large quite different from that of most Protestants, Jews and civil libertarians.

Even the Reverend John Courtney Murray, who was the leading liberal spokesman for the Roman Catholic Church on religious liberty and one of the chief authors of the Vatican Council Declaration on this subject, held a position far removed from most non-Catholic interpretations of religious liberty. In the foreword to his book *We Hold These Truths*, he stated:

> *The essays that follow . . . are also reflections of a Catholic who, in seeking his answer to the civil question, knows that the principles of Catholic faith and morality stand superior to, and in control of, the whole order of civil life. The question is sometimes raised, whether Catholicism is compatible with American democracy. The question is invalid as well as impertinent; for the manner of its position inverts the order of values. It must, of course, be turned around to read, whether American democracy is compatible with Catholicism.*[2]

It is the assumption of sectarian superiority or the assumption of a sectarian right to tap the public treasury that seems discriminatory and unjust to equally religious Americans of other faiths. These assumptions, which are not held by all Roman Catholics nor even by all priests, are nevertheless implicit in the political action being employed by the Roman Catholic hierarchy on matters relating to elementary and secondary education. That action since the Second Vatican Council apparently includes at least seven approaches.

The first is a papal reaffirmation of Canon Law 1381, which says:

> The religious training of youth in all schools whatever is subject to the authority and supervision of the Church. . . . The right and the duty vindicated in this canon are not restricted to schools established by the Church. The Church cannot renounce this right, since it is divinely conferred. . . .[3]

The January 12, 1967, Catholic *Register* printed a report originating in Vatican City under the headline "Pope Wants Catholic Education for All." The report said: "The Church must carry its efforts to all students, not just to Catholic schools and universities, a Papal letter has stated." The letter that the Pope sent to a Congress of the Inter-American Confederation of Catholic Education cited the Declaration on Christian Education of the Second Vatican Council in demanding "the cooperation of the family and the state. . . ."

The *Register* report emphasized the following in bold-face type:

> The letter further stated that while it is necessary to support and stimulate Catholic schools and universities, it is also necessary to carry the Gospel's message to all other students by means of competent Catholic teachers in public schools and by means of welfare projects and useful associations and centers to safeguard and develop the growth of Christian life.

This Papal letter to North and South Americans is apparently not an isolated case. *The New York Times* of April 13, 1967, reported from Bonn a Vatican note accusing the German "Government of violating the 1933 Concordat between the Holy See and Hitler's Third Reich." According to the same report

> Specific clauses of the concordat provide that the parochial schools would be built by the state when conditions warranted and that any disputes between the state and the church would be resolved by friendly negotiations.

In its note to the West German Government the Holy See was reported to have charged that both these clauses were being violated by the states' school reform laws. Rhineland–Palatinate and Baden–Wurtemberg adopted their school laws without prior consultation with the church, it said.

For many years there have been so-called "captive schools" in certain Roman Catholic dioceses in the United States. These are public schools that the Roman Catholic Church has been able to staff with teaching nuns, priests and brothers wearing their clerical garb. Religious symbols including statues of Catholic saints are in the classrooms and mass is said generally at the beginning of or just preceding the school day. Captive schools are public in the sense that all children of school age attend and all or most expenses are paid by taxes levied on the general public. But the real control is in the local Roman Catholic diocese.

These schools continue to exist in Kansas, Indiana, Illinois, Kentucky, Ohio, Texas and certain other states. There is no evidence that the hierarchy wants to extend this pattern to every community where there is a substantial Roman Catholic political influence. In fact, the shortage of nuns and priests would preclude this. But neither is there any evidence that the hierarchy as such is opposed to such control of the public schools. Generally speaking, where such schools have been removed from church control it has been as a result of court decisions or threat of court action. On the other hand, it is significant that a number of bishops have not taken advantage of political situations within their dioceses to take over public schools in this way.

The second and more important strategy being followed in the United States is that of trying almost everywhere to get as much indirect government aid as possible for parochial schools. Where such aid has been politically achieved the Roman Catholic bishops turn their attention to the securing of direct aid.

One of the chief forms of indirect aid is public bus service to parochial schools. The aims of both conservative and progressive bishops appear to be the same. It is in the tactics or method of operation that differences appear.

In Pennsylvania the full weight of the Roman Catholic hierarchy was openly thrown into the battle to influence the legislature.

"The campaign was started by Archbishop John J. Krol of the Archdiocese of Philadelphia," according to the July 3, 1963, Pittsburgh *Post Gazette*, which reported "an organized Catholic effort to win state-financed school bus transportation" to parochial schools. So much pressure was put on the governor and legislators that the bill, which had the support of Governor Scranton, was being rushed to a vote without a public hearing of opponents, who did not know in advance of the secretly planned campaign. The reason given by some committee members to the Reverend George Evans of the State Council of Churches, for refusing opponents a chance to be heard, was that a public hearing would delay and kill the bill since the adjournment of the legislature was scheduled for July 31, 1963.

The bill actually was defeated in the 1963 session of the legislature because of opposition of Protestant groups and also of Senator Paul S. Wagner, chairman of the Senate education committee.

The Roman Catholic hierarchy and lay Catholic groups like Citizens for Educational Freedom took quick reprisal. A campaign was mounted against Senator Wagner, who was defeated in the November, 1964, election. A spokesman for Citizens for Educational Freedom took credit for the loss of a lot of votes by the Senator, who as a Republican, would normally have been reelected. The landslike vote for President Johnson may actually, however, have contributed more to the defeat of Senator Wagner than the school bus issue.

In Erie, the third largest city in the state where 65 per cent of the people are Roman Catholics, there was a year-long campaign aimed at defeating Senator William G. Sesler. Sesler had voted against the parochial school bus bill in 1963. On October 14, 1964, *The Patriot*, published in Harrisburg, the state capital, reported in a dispatch from Erie that "priests in some parishes spoke out from the pulpit. The upshot was that a candidate without any political backing, Charles Schmitt, ran up an extraordinary 7,423 vote total to Sesler's 11,457 in the Democratic primary." *The Patriot* also reported "in these last weeks before the election" that

speeches on "The Bus Bill" are being made before Catholic

groups throughout the Erie area by such prominent church figures as Monsignor Alfred Watson, vicar general of the diocese, and Monsignor Homer Dewalt, superintendent of the Erie parochial school system. One prominent Erie man, a leading Catholic layman, says that "in my 35 adult years I have never seen the church here become involved in a political campaign this way."

When the election was over Sesler had won, riding in on the Johnson landslide. *The Patriot* pointed out that the hierarchy's campaign "is backfiring in Sesler's favor, especially in the heavily Protestant rural areas outside Erie city." But the tough reprisal approach of the hierarchy had its effect. On November 5 the Philadelphia *Evening Bulletin* reported one observer as saying "that as a result of Tuesday's election the Republican-controlled State Senate would appear to be favorably disposed towards the legislation while in the Democratic-controlled House, he said, 'I don't see how it could miss.' "

It didn't miss. The work of William Ball, director and general counsel for the Pennsylvania Catholic Welfare Committee, the hierarchy and Citizens for Educational Freedom produced a favorable vote in both houses in spite of a well-run campaign against the bill by The Friends of the Public Schools.

Opponents of the bill reported that even with such activity on the part of the Roman Catholic Church the bill might not have passed if Governor Scranton had not used the full power of his patronage to whip senators into line.

So eager was the hierarchy to show its strength and to get financial support for those sending their children to parochial schools that the ecumenical spirit went out the window in Pennsylvania even during the Vatican Council sessions. One prominent Protestant churchman told this writer that the Philadelphia archdiocese rejected an overture for dialogue about the problem.

Pennsylvania was not an isolated instance. In Ohio, where similar bus legislation was at stake, the Dayton *Journal Herald* reported on October 29, 1964, that a Roman Catholic, John J. Dugan, who was a candidate for the legislature, attacked the Catholic school system for its political activity. "The Catholic school system is making a great mistake by using its facilities, including nuns and teachers, to distribute literature endorsing candidates for public office," said Dugan.

In contrast to this official use of Roman Catholic power to achieve institutional gains, a somewhat different method to achieve the same objective was used in Missouri prior to 1966. The Missouri bishops, some of whom are considered progressives, decided to leave the political campaign for parochial school buses to laymen. *The Catholic Layman* for July, 1963, described their decision in these words

> *Missouri's Catholic parents are writing a new chapter in U.S. Church history—one that is certain to have national impact. For the first time, Missouri's bishops refused to put Catholic support behind proposed state legislation of the type traditionally backed by Church spokesmen and organizations.*
>
> *Their decision not to work for adoption of a bill to permit tax-paid school bus rides for parochial school children was in sharp contrast to their attitude of a decade ago when they and official Catholic organizations bombarded the state capital with telegrams and statements on a similar bill.*
>
> *In speeches and in response to inquiries about their new stand, the bishops agreed to say something like this: "This is the age of the layman. Your mission—not ours—is to work in the world. If you want the school bus bill, get it yourselves. If not, okay."*
>
> *The result was slow in coming and observers thought for a long time that the parents did not understand. But then, when it fully dawned on them what was happening, the result was the nationally publicized mass transfers of parochial pupils to protest the Legislature's killing of the bus bill.*
>
> The bishops reportedly will maintain their stand: parents will carry the ball.

Throughout the 1963 legislative campaign for parochial school bus service in Missouri, the bishops with a few exceptions were not directly involved in pressure on the legislature. Bishop Charles Helmsing issued a public release, May 6, 1963, in which he called the Missouri legislature's defeat of the parochial school bus bill "a grave injustice." When the House Judiciary Committee refused to report out the bus bill and the House refused to override its committee, Roman Catholic parochial school children swarmed into the public schools of Jefferson City, without previous notice, as did at least 1750 parochial school pupils in St. Louis. In the absence of Bishop Helmsing, a public statement by Monsignor William Baum, subsequently executive director of the Bishop's Commission for Ecumenical Affairs, to the effect that he knew of no similar demonstrations being planned in Kansas City, had the effect of discouraging parochial school transfers in Kansas City though a few did take place in suburban areas.

After the demonstrations had begun, spokesmen for some of the Roman Catholic bishops indicated that the demonstrations had occurred without their knowledge. Cardinal Joseph E. Ritter's office said he neither approved nor disapproved of the movement, which he felt was a protest by parents and not a church matter.

Dr. Stanley I. Stuber, then executive secretary of the Missouri Council of Churches, who had hoped the Second Vatican Council would lead to different Church–State assumptions, sent the following telegram to the Missouri bishops: "Many feel these irresponsible protests against the vote of the Missouri House judiciary committee could not take place without the official sanction of the church." Bishop Helmsing subsequently released a statement to the press which included a provocative sentence: "While I hate to see peace disrupted, we cannot have peace at any cost and especially at the cost of injustice." Bishop Helmsing's diocesan newspaper *The Catholic Reporter,* although in favor of the bus bill, did not campaign for it and even questioned the tone of an editorial in the Jefferson City diocesan paper, *The Catholic Missourian.* That editorial had asserted that those on the House Judiciary Committee who voted against the bill "must someday appear before the judgment seat of God to give an accounting for their actions." It spoke of the "inevitable" sentence Christ would pronounce against the members of that committee.

When further legislative hearings were held on a proposal to amend the state constitution, it was obvious to any objective observer that the full weight of the Missouri bishops was not being thrown into the legislative battle. On the other hand, it is clear that at least some of the bishops felt compelled to speak forcefully for the measure even while trying to keep hands off direct supervision of the movement. The bishops of course were not neutral. Five priests in Missouri individually told this writer they were opposed to the bus bill but did not dare say so publicly. Priests who favored it, however, were free to encourage laymen, though few actually entered into the public press with public statements.

It was Citizens for Educational Freedom and the Knights of Columbus who spearheaded the campaign both in 1963 and in 1964–65.

It is difficult to assess the virtue in one method of aiding parochial schools as against the other.

In Missouri, where only 16 or 17 per cent of the people are Roman Catholic, the pressure methods of the hierarchy could not have had quite the same effect as in Pennsylvania. Certainly the effort by Citizens for Educational Freedom to appear independent and nonsectarian deceived no one but the few Protestants who had been induced to join. The overwhelming majority of its members are militant Roman Catholics. It receives consistently more space in diocesan newspapers than any other allegedly nonsectarian group in the United States. The National Catholic Education Association's superintendents adopted a resolution during their 1965 convention endorsing CEF and promising it all possible support.[4] In Kansas City the first diocesan school board to include lay people was confronted with a decision on whether parish parent teachers associations should be expected to work with CEF. The decision was to leave to parish PTAs their relationships with CEF.[5]

A similar effort was being pursued in Ohio. Following conferences between Roman Catholic bishops, Governor James A. Rhodes, State Senate Majority Leader Theodore M. Gray and others, the Republicans decided to aid parochial schools. The Cleveland *Press* of Thursday, July 13, 1967, stated that "on Monday Rhodes was host at another of his occasional unannounced lunches for the state's Roman Catholic bishops." It also reported that the Republicans, in a political effort to force Democrats to vote for a big tax increase, will combine taxes with a school appropriation bill containing aid to parochial schools."

A third approach is that of trying to remove constitutional

restrictions on direct and indirect aid to parochial schools.

During 1966 and 1967 a key battle was fought to delete from the New York State constitution Article XI, Section 3. This section provided that "neither the state nor any subdivision thereof shall use . . . any . . . public money . . . directly or indirectly in aid or maintenance . . . of any school or institution of learning wholly or in part under the control or direction of any religious denomination, or in which any denominational tenet or doctrine is taught."

The struggle to control the state constitutional convention began in 1966 when delegates were elected. On November 10, 1966, the Brooklyn *Tablet*, the diocesan newspaper of Brooklyn, claimed that 106 of the 186 delegates had committed themselves in advance to eliminate Article XI, Section 3, from the constitution. So effective had been the advance planning that Assembly Speaker Anthony J. Travia, who was designated president of the constitutional convention, asserted: "I feel that repeal of the Blaine Amendment was a foregone conclusion before the convention opened."[6]

Public opposition to deletion, however, was so great that the hierarchy felt a continuing political effort was necessary. Twenty groups, among which were the United Parents Association, the United Federation of Teachers, the American Jewish Congress, the New York State Council of Churches, Americans for Democratic Action and the New York Civil Liberties Union, joined forces in a Committee for Public Education and Religious Liberty, to oppose repeal of Article XI, Section 3.

The Roman Catholic campaign to bring pressure to bear for repeal involved "a series of mass parish meetings throughout a ten-county area" under Cardinal Spellman's supervision. Spellman called this fight over the amendment "the gravest crisis in the history of the Catholic Church in America." On June 1, 1967, the Rockland County *Journal News,* in reporting this activity, indicated that "parents were present [at parish meetings] in response to a Diocesan letter brought home by their school age children." The letter, according to the newspaper, "required parental attendance." The *Journal News* also reported that "a film prepared by the Archdiocese was shown in nearly every parish. It detailed the financial and personnel crisis facing the Church today. . . ." The same newspaper added: "Discussion in some parishes reached heights of emotion, prompting pastors to warn that the outcome of the referendum 'may mean the life or death of the Catholic Church in America.' " Parents, the report said, were also "urged, sometimes told, to join a national interdenominational lobbying group, Citizens for Educational Freedom. . . ."

In Brooklyn, the diocesan paper *The Tablet* reported on June 15, 1967, that " 'Fairness to Children' committees are being formed in each of the 225 parishes of the Diocese." These committees, which "will consist of seven members: a priest, a Sister and Brother" and "representatives of other active parish organizations" will "conduct a campaign to have people register and vote in November," when the proposed constitution was expected to be up for final adoption.

As a result of the hierarchy's campaign the constitutional convention voted 132 to 49 to repeal the state's ban against financial aid to church-supported schools. An attempted compromise in the form of an amendment to authorize shared time programs while retaining a ban on direct public financial aid to church-supported schools was defeated.[7]

Church authorities were unable to prevent the adoption of an amendment prohibiting racial and religious discrimination in admissions to schools supported by public funds. A Fordham law professor was reported in *The New York Times* of August 18, 1967, as expressing fear that such an amendment would destroy the Roman Catholic school system. This was apparently not its intent and there is no evidence that many non-Catholics would seek parochial school education if public schools received adequate support and were thus able to maintain good academic standards.

Prior to the vote by the people of New York on the new constitution, the campaign for and against passage hinged largely on the question whether the constitution should sanction public aid to church schools. The constitutional convention had refused to submit this issue separately to the voters. When the popular vote was taken on November 7, 1967, the proposed constitution was defeated by a margin of more than 2½ to 1. The defeat was attributed to the strong feeling that the concept of separation of church and state should not be eroded. The vote, however, was not along religious lines, since a number of heavily Roman Catholic districts turned out substantial majorities against the proposed constitution. "One political leader," according to the November 9, 1967, *New York Times*, "said he found Catholics resenting pressures" from the hierarchy "that seemed to them almost to foreclose the right to decide how to vote."

The fourth approach is that of securing direct aid either to parochial schools or to children in the form of tuition grants.

In Pennsylvania, House Bill 2170 was introduced during the 1967 legislative sessions to provide for a "State Nonpublic School Authority Act" under which an annual appropriation would be made for sectarian schools. The bill included language typical of those seeking aid to parochial schools during recent years. It referred, for example, to the money saved Pennsylvania taxpayers each year by parochial schools and indicated "that nonpublic schools, through providing instruction in secular subjects, make an important contribution to the achieving of such public purpose." It also asserted, in line with CEF demands and the Vatican Council Declaration on Education, that "freedom to choose a nonpublic school, meeting reasonable state standards for a child, is a fundamental parental liberty and a basic right," thus identifying religious liberty with state aid. The technique being used is that of persuading the legislature "to enter into contracts for the purchase of services with persons or institutions whether public or nonpublic, sectarian or nonsectarian."

The bill even restates traditional Church claims that if parochial school parents should "remove their children to the public schools of the Commonwealth, an intolerable added financial burden to the public would result. . . ."

The Philadelphia *Sunday Bulletin* of July 16, 1967, reported that CEF was behind the bill and also indicated that officials of the Philadelphia Archdiocese had set up an organization to spearhead the campaign. According to the *Sunday Bulletin*, "lay committees were formed in each parish to disseminate information about the legislation and to ask for support of the letter-writing campaign." As a result of the campaign fifty thousand letters had been mailed to the governor and legislators, according to the same paper.

The church bulletin of St. Dorothy's Roman Catholic Church,

Burmant Road and Township Line, Drexel Hill, Pennsylvania, carried the following announcement on Sunday, July 9, 1967, asking "prompt action" on "the Nonpublic School Authority Bill":

> *To prevent a delay, and for your convenience in getting your reaction into the hands of your representatives, you will find— at the church doors—form letters which merely require the name and address of your representative, and your name and address. If you wish, you may send your own personal letters. We urge mailing at the earliest possible date, and ask that you send the tear off form to Robert J. Sims with the information for his records.*

Sims is the layman whom the Philadelphia *Sunday Bulletin* reported "was asked by officials of the Archdiocese to head the drive." The tear sheet to be sent to him listed the governor and three state representatives and asked the name and address of the Catholic layman sending the sheet and a report on whether he had written to each of these.

The bill as finally adopted on June 17, 1968, provides for the financing from horse racing revenue of parochial school textbooks, salaries for teachers and teaching aides in mathematics, physical education, physical science and foreign languages. The campaign to secure adoption was planned and executed by the Pennsylvania Catholic Conference, with the lead being taken by Cardinal John Krol of Philadelphia, but Roman Catholic leaders view horse racing revenue as inadequate and therefore a necessary compromise to get legislation adopted.

In Missouri a similar strategy of aid to parochial schools was developing. The St. Louis *Post Dispatch* of January 1, 1967, stated: "Formation of a Missouri Catholic Conference was announced by the Catholic bishops of the state". It is the state and national Catholic Welfare Conferences that manage the political activity for the hierarchy. Only a few months prior to this announcement, the Kansas City *Star*, on October 20, 1966, reported that "Catholic parents and teachers of the Kansas City–St. Joseph Diocese last night were urged to swing their political weight in the November 8 political election." The same paper reported the adoption of a "resolution recommending that PTA committees in each school get acquainted with their legislative and judicial candidates in the next two weeks and hold general meetings to acquaint their members 'with the attitudes of the candidates on issues affecting private school students, teachers and parents.' "

Officials of the diocese had earlier asked the Governor's Conference on Education for state tuition grants to parents with children in parochial schools and for other parochial school aid. Diocesan leaders spoke to parish and other Catholic groups to which state legislators and congressmen had been invited. They told those assembled of the importance of government aid to parochial schools.[8]

Prior to the November 8, 1966, election, sample ballots were sent by mail to Roman Catholic adults throughout the diocese by Citizens for Educational Freedom and were distributed in at least a few churches Sunday morning. The sample printed ballots varied district by district throughout the diocese since more than thirty House seats and a number of Senate seats in the Missouri legislature were at stake. Judges who did not agree with the CEF position had a "No" recommendation at the point where the ballot asked if they were to be retained in office.

It seems obvious from these various reports that there is a widespread political effort designed to achieve public support for parochial schools. The support demanded is no longer in the form of fringe benefits or indirect aid but ranges from tuition grants to public funds for purchase of educational services, another way of phrasing direct aid.

While such activity seems to be the main political thrust of the hierarchy (there has been no such concerted effort on behalf of civil rights or other legislation, for example), there are a number of bishops who do not promote such programs. On January 26, 1964, the Boston *Globe* for example, reported an address of Cardinal Cushing at Sudsbury Methodist Church in which he said:

Once you have religion tied up with a state, religion is going to come out in second place.

We have to live within the letter and the spirit of the Constitution.

Once a state or government starts financing church-related schools or a church-related system of education, the next step is a controlled system.

A fifth approach is also being used by some Roman Catholic leaders. This is the ecumenical appeal. It links the new effort at dialogue and understanding with other efforts to silence Protestants and Jews or get support from them for public aid to parochial schools. The April 23, 1967, Philadelphia *Inquirer* reported that Archbishop John J. Krol "made a passionate bid Saturday for Protestant backing in the effort to get public aid for parochial schools." He used the first formal ecumenical opportunity before Philadelphia Protestants for this appeal. The *Inquirer* said: "In a speech marking the first official appearance of a Roman Catholic prelate at a meeting of the Greater Philadelphia Council of Churches," Krol declared: "I come to you today, then, as a beggar, a beggar for the parochial schools that mean so much not just to me but the parents and the children and the teachers who have devoted their lives to this work."

Krol said "that organized religion has been a major contributor to 'the crisis' in America's church-related schools." By "crisis" he meant "humanistic secularism," which he called "a form of religion which by our default has become the established religion in our country." He appealed to the Protestants to participate in a "new beginning, a first step in what must be a continuing dialogue" about parochial education.

While Archbishop Krol was using the ecumenical spirit as a lever to get aid for the Roman Catholic Church, New York Catholic leaders were using another method to exploit the ecumenical mood. They called the amendment they wanted to delete from the New York constitution "the Blaine Amendment." Blaine was a senator from Maine who is believed to have lost the Presidential election in 1884 because one of his supporters, Samuel D. Burchard, used an anti-Catholic slogan: "Rum, Romanism, and Rebellion."

"By use of the name [Blaine]," said the New York Civil Liberties Union, "advocates of aid to parochial schools hope to pin an anti-Catholic label on opponents of aid to parochial schools." This was a device, said one Protestant leader to this writer, to keep ecumenical-minded Protestants from opposing the Catholic campaign, for how could anyone be ecumenical and anti-Catholic at the same time?

In point of fact, it was Elihu Root, not Blaine, who wrote the amendment. "A similar provision," said the New York Civil Liberties Union "has been part of New York law since 1844 when James G. Blaine was only 14. It was incorporated in the Constitution in 1894, more than a year after Blaine died." The amendment is attributed by parochial school spokesmen to Blaine on a "guilt by association basis" because Blaine was one of many supporters of a similarly worded amendment to the federal Constitution. The amendment of course is not directed specifically against the Roman Catholic Church but against the establishment of any religion.

The same exploitation of ecumenism has been used elsewhere, although not generally recorded in the public press. In a large midwestern city where negotiations were under way to include Roman Catholics in the local Council of Churches, word was quietly passed around that the price for such ecumenical cooperation was Protestant soft-pedaling of opposition to aid to parochial schools.

It is worth noting that the exploitation of the ecumenical spirit for institutional purposes may be simply a sign of the desperation of those who have the responsibility of financing the hundreds of schools and other church enterprises in their jurisdiction. It is certainly not evidence, as some assert in extreme statements, that the ecumenical movement is a device for the achievement of aid to parochial schools. The ecumenical emphasis within the Roman Catholic Church has a validity of its own. Every denomination has its "imperialists," its conservatives, its progressives and even those who believe the institution stands in the way of the genuine religious life. It is unfortunate that in any church the institutionalists often tend to become bishops, or that some bishops tend to become institutionalists.

A sixth approach being considered in some quarters is much less dependent on public funds, yet does imply certain special relationships between church schools and public schools. This approach is apparently being pushed on an experimental basis in Swanton, Vermont. The *Christian Science Monitor* of March 14, 1967, reports that the Reverend John R. LaBrake, formerly principal of Swanton's parochial school, is the project director of a federally financed center that will combine religious and non-religious school facilities. A grant from the U.S. Office of Education in the amount of "$56,000, not only pays Father LaBrake's salary, and the salaries of any staff he hires but may be used to 'sell' the project to the voters."

Father LaBrake organized the idea of a new school complex that would cost three million dollars and would include under the same roof a religious school. The February, 1967, *School Management* referred to this as a proposal for "a consolidated junior-senior, public-parochial school. . . ."

Father LaBrake has stated that the religious school would be privately constructed, owned and staffed. "According to Father LaBrake," said the *Christian Science Monitor*, "any denomination will be free to use the school" but "it will be owned by the local Roman Catholic parish."

School Management reports LaBrake as indicating that the religious center

> will offer both denominational and "ecumenical" instruction—as elective, noncredit courses. It may also offer a parochial diploma—under the Ste. Anne's Academy charter—to youngsters who spend half of their school day in the center under Catholic tutelage. In effect the center will operate as Ste. Anne's high school . . . while the present Ste. Anne's Academy plant will be limited to elementary school instruction.

Plans call for classrooms, offices for religious advisers and a chapel for formal religious services as well as informal use.

The *Christian Science Monitor* editorially assailed the U.S. Office of Education for "promoting a development which unquestionably violates the spirit of the First Amendment's requirements for a separation of church and state and may conceivably violate the letter . . . as well." The *Monitor* added: "Although public funds will not be used in the operation of this school, its very nearness will lend it an official and public standing which clearly violates the spirit of the First Amendment."

The *Monitor* editorial spelled out further this merging of the public and the church school by stating that "the local Catholic parochial school will be enabled to close down its present costly facilities, send its pupils to the public school, secure in the knowledge that they need but step into an adjoining wing of the school for religious instruction."

The Swanton plan is really a logical extension of shared time. It is based on a partnership philosophy that those churches that operate weekday church schools are to have a unique relationship with public schools, with other denominations being permitted the use of the chapel, offices and classroom. Even if all denominations were included on an equal basis the exclusion of humanist and nonreligious societies that wanted to participate in the educational program would be clearly discriminatory. Unless it is assumed that the United States is a religious instead of a secular community, there is no reason why the John Birch Society, the Socialist Party, the American Legion, a pacifist organization and a society to promote atheism would not be legally entitled to an office, classroom and school time under the Swanton plan. They would obviously not be entitled to such facilities in a building belonging to religious groups, but they ought to have the right to the same proximity to the public school.

If, however, final plans for construction of the Swanton school do not include connecting facilities or the housing of both public and parochial schools under one roof, much of the objection to the Swanton program would be removed. If all religious groups and any nonreligious groups that wanted to use a portion of the school day were equally permitted to have a noncredit course in lieu of study hall, the rest of the objection would be removed.

One other approach to religious education which does not necessarily involve government financial aid or a merging of public and private schools seems to have the support of both Protestants and Roman Catholics and may also receive some Jewish approval. This is the Columbia, Maryland, proposal, which originated outside the Roman Catholic Church.

The Columbia proposal provides for a minimum of one school period for each of five days for each child enrolled in the religious education program. The religious educational agencies will provide jointly through a Religious Facilities Corporation a building or mobile classroom adjacent to but presumably not a part of the public school building. The same agencies plan to employ professionally trained teachers wherever possible.

Presumably this proposal is constitutional under the terms of the Zorach decision involving released time. If an hour each day throughout a child's school life is available, neither parochial schools nor shared time is involved. No group would be excluded from a released time arrangement even though some might have to find other housing than that provided by the Religious Facilities Corporation.

The Columbia proposal has been encouraged by the Roman Catholic Archdiocese of Baltimore, the National Council of Churches and twelve Protestant denominations.

In the January 20, 1967, diocesan paper *The Catholic Reporter,* the Reverend John P. Cole of the Kansas City–St. Joseph Diocese, as has already been suggested, outlined essentially the Columbia plan, although privately he has also commended the Swanton plan. In his article he indicated that

> *For years [public schools] have been associated in the Roman Catholic mind with the Protestant ethic. But this too has been changing. More and more the public schools are becoming truly secular. The famous Bible reading and prayer decisions of the Supreme Court are just two evidences of this. It is evident that the public school endeavor is not that of providing even a bland kind of religious formation. Its role is to teach the secular sciences and the values inherent in them. But given public support and preserving separation of church and state, perhaps it is feasible that all of the prime educational time need not be preempted by general education.*

Neither the Columbia plan nor the parallel statements by a few educator-priests like Father Cole have received much publicity. Yet they point the way to a different educational strategy that can avoid the major Church–State problems of government support of religious education and preferential status to parochial schools on the one hand, and on the other hand permit ecumenical cooperation in providing religious classes outside the public school, thus maintaining the integrity of secular education for all.

The openness of the Baltimore Archdiocese to the Columbia plan is an indication that no one final strategy with respect to religious education has been adopted by the hierarchy. The well-publicized efforts of the bishops in such states as New York and Pennsylvania together with CEF and other activity in other states may therefore not be indicative of the mood of the whole Church.

From the standpoint of the entire Church but especially the Roman Catholic Church, future strategy with respect to education is crucial. If the Roman Catholic Church succeeds in getting substantial government aid for its schools it is virtually certain that it will indefinitely be bound to parochial schools, with most of its trained personnel tied to those schools. If the Church avoids such government aid by a different approach to education it will free both personnel and funds for more creative experimentation in various religious and secular community projects.

Moreover, the whole question of respect for the right of citizens not to be taxed for support of Church projects is integrally connected with respect for personality, without which no church can merit the affection of those outside its own membership.

Conclusion

It is apparent that twentieth-century America faces many problems in connection with religious liberty. These problems have arisen out of the pluralist nature of our society and have been intensified by two developments: the welfare state and the increasing emphasis on the secular. The executive and legislative branches of the federal government have offered government funds to church schools and colleges, ostensibly to promote the welfare aims of the State, while the Supreme Court has declared that any act of government must have "a secular legislative purpose and a primary effect that neither advances nor inhibits religion." Yet the public record shows that the President, Congress and various state legislatures were not proposing government aid to religious institutions for secular reasons but chiefly because of the political power exercised by those churches seeking public funds.

Aside from the motivation of government bodies there is the question of the primary effect of such aid. It is one of the theses of this book that the subsidy of a school or a program whose only reason for existence is to provide religious education, directly benefits the religious purpose that created and sustains the school or program. Almost every religious institution has some secular activity even if it is no more than the providing of a room where a Boy Scout troop meets. It is impossible, however, to subsidize the "Boy Scout room" in a church without subsidizing the church by that much. If the government wants to subsidize the Boy Scouts instead of the church it could provide a separate Boy Scout building. The fact is significant that the government has not asked churches to provide secular education but that some churches have asked government to subsidize their educational projects.

Throughout much of American history two forces combined to prevent government subsidy of church enterprises. The first of these was the whole spirit of voluntary giving and private philanthropy. This element, while still present, is being challenged by the availability of government funds for almost anything politically powerful groups want. For example, throughout most of American history neither Protestant nor Roman Catholic colleges thought of the government as a source of support.

The second force was a combination of Protestant–Roman Catholic rivalry and the fact that parochial schools were the principal mechanism whereby Roman Catholics maintained their distinctiveness in a largely Protestant culture. As a result of Protestant dominance it was impossible for the government to give financial preference to Roman Catholic institutions.

Today, with the rising cost of living, building construction and equipment, both Protestants and Roman Catholics are seeking government funds. The religious recipients of public funds are at one and the same time trying to make a case for being secular enough to get government support and religious enough to get church support. Their secular claim is that some of their buildings or equipment are used for teaching essentially secular subjects. Yet faculty, students, curriculum, tuition and other funds are part of an integrated religious educational system.

One of the authors of a recent study of parochial education indicates that "there is no doubt that the parochial schools represent useful recruiting grounds for the clergy and the religious orders. Teaching sisters and priests scan the student body care-

fully for signs of vocation, and often the measure of a good parochial school is not how many achieve success in the secular world
but how many take the vows of poverty and chastity."[1]

The secular by-products of parochial schools are incidental to
the main or religious thrust in other areas as well. No one can
argue with the right of any church to use its religious educational system for recruiting for the ministry or for other uniquely
religious matters. One can, however, point out that the general
public ought not to be taxed to subsidize any part of a religiously
integrated school on the allegation or assumption that a part of
it is secular.

It seems patently contradictory and unjust for the judicial
branch of government to forbid the use of public devotional
exercises or worship in public schools while the President, Congress and state legislatures use public funds to subsidize church
schools where worship and religious indoctrination are central.
The injustice is that of unequal treatment since if the use of
public funds requires a public and hence a secular purpose in
one set of schools it should in another as well.

There is yet another injustice perpetuated by government in
granting aid to church enterprises, and this is that such aid en-
courages the church to use political power for its private gain.
The result is that some church authorities try to prevent any
increase in taxes or public support for public schools while
trying to get a chunk of public funds for parochial schools.
Peter and Alice Rossi, who have made a study of parochial school
education, have concluded that "in cities in which the Catholics
form the majority, the kind of financial and political support for
good public school education may often seem jeopardized by that
fact alone."[2] One of the reasons the hierarchy is so successful in
limiting the financial support of public schools is the fact that
"the parent who has sent his children to the parochial school
manifests a low degree of concern for public schools."[3]

If in the future many Protestant elementary and secondary
schools should be built and subsidized by the government, the
outlook for public education would be very dim. Protestants no
less than Roman Catholics are motivated by self-interest, a by-
product of which is often apathy about others. Even now in such
a traditionally Protestant center as Kansas City, Missouri, Protes-

tants were tax-conscious and apathetic in the face of efforts by
other groups to defeat a public school tax levy in the 1966
general elections.

In the final analysis government neutrality in religious matters
does not and cannot depend on the assumption that Protestants
are irrevocably devoted to separation of Church and State or
that the Roman Catholic Church since the Second Vatican Council is concerned about religious liberty. Both groups are likely
to be governed by self-interest when their own institutional interests are at stake.

One answer to the self-interest of the major churches is that the
unchurched, the Jews and the civil libertarian groups must serve
as a watchdog and restraining influence when churches seek public funds. But from the standpoint of the Church this is an inadequate answer. The Church must have a clearer understanding of
the State than it does and a clearer understanding of its own
theological position.

The Church and the State have a co-responsibility for the
achieving of justice and for encouraging individuals to participate
in the political process. But this co-responsibility does not mean
that Church and State are political partners in the sense that they
jointly assume immediate responsibility for a particular economic
system or political program. The Church fails in its responsibility
if it becomes the agent of the State to promote the general welfare, just as the State fails if it becomes the agent of the Church
to promote or finance the Church's work in society.

The modern tendency of the Church is quite different from the
medieval tendency. Today the Church is tempted not so much to
control the State as to cooperate with the State for the advancement of specific goals. This is possible only in a benevolent State.
It is all the more important for the Church to realize that a
benevolent State perverts the purpose of religion quite as much as
the hostile State.

In modern America the Church, in spite of its theology, tends
not to see itself as over against the State but as ancillary to it,
as a teammate in the effort to achieve moderate social justice.
The State, however, defines the context, provides the money and
sets the rules. In this context the Church's conflict with the State
does not come over issues of social justice but over the degree

of independence the Church is to have while administering government projects or funds.

The proper function of the Church with respect to the State is to remind it of its purpose and task of preserving and enhancing human life, to point the direction but not to become either a partner or subordinate agency in the normal work of government.

The proper function of the State with respect to the Church is to provide an atmosphere free from injustice, prejudice, discrimination and persecution in which the Church may not only worship but be prophetic.

The distinction must be kept between Christians sharing in the tasks of the State as citizens and the Church doing the work of the State. The Church is to clarify, not to usurp, the functions of the State, to insist on the proper means being used to fulfill them and to challenge the abuse or misuse of power. The only time when the Church should engage in tasks that are properly the function of government is when the State will not perform its duty or does it inadequately.

The fundamental issue with respect to education between most Protestants and Roman Catholics is whether education is basically the function of secular society or basically the function of the Church. One need not be "anti-Catholic" to hold that education is primarily a function of secular society. In fact, many Roman Catholics hold essentially the same view. The very fact that Roman Catholic leaders have accepted dual school enrollment even on a provisional basis is evidence of some acceptance of the valid role of secular society in education.

Although many Protestants are presumably committed to secular education, neither the major Protestant churches nor the Roman Catholic Church have been very concerned with the millions of children who have poor schools or no opportunity to go beyond high school. The Roman Catholic Church has provided almost no leadership in updating public education because it has been too interested in its own schools. The Protestant churches have likewise done very little, although for a different reason. Protestant concern for the public schools has been largely seen in terms of defense of the system as it is by preventing the division of public funds between two systems. The task of both branches of Christianity and of Judaism is to propose major advances in public education in addition to advancing their own educational and institutional interests.

For example, no church has engaged in significant action to raise the salaries of public school teachers. There is little chance of improving the nation's schools unless our society is prepared to offer an adequate wage to those to whom they entrust their children for twelve years.

No church has worked to assure every child in America of a chance to attend a nursery school for at least half a day where he can learn motor skills, receive health care, etc. Many children of the poor are two to three years behind other children because they do not have access to such tools as crayons, paper and toys that teach coordination.

No church has campaigned on a state level for a system of community colleges so that every person in the state would be within reasonable commuting distance of free higher education.

The failure of churches adequately to support and extend public education undoubtedly can be laid to a general apathy toward social issues as well as to a greater concern for their own institutional interests. In this context it is appropriate to suggest that the ability of the churches to make a significant contribution to public education depends in large part upon not having rival institutional claims upon the public treasury.

If the prophetic function of encouraging social change is jeopardized by dependence on government funds, so also is the church's liberty at other points. The American Civil Liberties Union has wisely indicated that when government can grant or withhold its support of religious institutions it has the "power to distort the directions of religious activity."

The strange paradox confronting the Church is this: it can preserve its own liberty only by defending the liberty of those who do not want either to join or support it. An all-wise Creator has apparently made the universe in such a way that religious institutions as well as other forms of social organization cannot escape the judgment that follows from compelling people to support externally that which they cannot accept inwardly.

The reliance of religious institutions on government support necessarily involves the coercion of nonbelievers through taxes to pay for a faith that they do not accept. But as unwilling contributors they have the right to influence the direction of public expenditures and the institutions dependent upon public funds. A free Church is thus apparently dependent upon maintaining freedom from the control of nonbelievers and hence from dependence on secular government. If this is true, the free exercise of religion is necessarily dependent upon avoiding an establishment of religion.

The avoidance of an establishment of religion is also essential to the free exercise of religion in another way. If the nonreligious citizen is to be truly free from having to support religious institutions he must not be taxed for Church purposes. In this way a truly secular government and a secular school system are the civil counterparts of the religious assumption that each man and his conscience must be treated with respect.

The Church and genuine religion are endangered only when they seek to destroy or manipulate the secular in the interest of safeguarding or extending their own interests. Paradoxically, the group that is least concerned with its own institution is more likely to preserve it, if only because it wins the admiration and affection of the people for whom it spends itself in serving. Sometimes it is suggested that churches and religious liberty in England have not been jeopardized by government support or by the teaching of religion in the schools. It is true that the government itself does not interfere with the churches except at certain points concerning the Anglican Church. But popular respect for the churches is at a low ebb in British life. The churches have permitted and encouraged the use of secular educational institutions for religious purposes, with the result that a bland religion, or a small inoculation, has served to reduce both the meaning of religion and the influence of the churches.

If the Church is to be vital it must not only see the value in the secular state and secular school but engage in vital service and action to improve the entire secular society. The success of any religious faith, of any church, is not evident in the religious symbols that decorate the public places of the secular society nor in the public acceptance of religious worship as cultural ritual, nor even in the penetration of public institutions with formal doctrinal teaching, all of which were a part of many pre-Communist Eastern European societies and are today a part of

Latin America and such Western European countries as Italy, where economic and social justice are seriously lacking. The success of religious faith is evident in the respect with which any society treats its poorest citizen, in the justice accorded equally to all and in the concern for all people in other nations as well. As Leo Pfeffer said to a group of Christians in 1964: "What people want is justice, not charity." They want as a matter of right what is often dispensed as a gift.

Justice of course is a by-product of love or respect for persons. In the truest sense, justice is possible only when there is genuine community. It is this genuine community on a worldwide basis which is true ecumenism. Ecumenism is not to be confused with institutional church mergers but with a unity of faith that seeks to create a human community of love and justice.

This writer, who has been a part of meaningful and much-valued experiences in ecumenical dialogue in recent years, has in every experience felt that the ecumenical movement and the cause of true religion can be served only by frankness and open discussion of differences, and an honest effort to surmount them. The problems of Church, State, and education are not insurmountable and the quality of both American religious and educational life demands a serious effort by Americans of all faiths and of none to cooperate in solving them.

Notes

CHAPTER 1

[1] Quoted in Anson Phelps Stokes, *Church and State in the United States* (New York: Harper, 1950), I, 142.

[2] Leo Pfeffer, *Church, State and Freedom* (Boston: Beacon, 1953), p. 98.

[3] *Ibid.*, p. 100.

[4] *Ibid.*, p. 101.

[5] *Ibid.*, p. 115.

[6] Charles Beard, *The Republic* (New York: Viking, 1944), p. 166.

[7] *Congressional Globe*, 39th Cong., 1st Sess., p. 2765.

[8] *Ibid.*

[9] *Ibid.*, pp. 1088–90. See also *Congressional Globe*, 42nd Cong., 1st Sess., Appendix, p. 150, where Bingham restated his intention in drafting the 14th Amendment.

[10] 330 U.S. 1 at 15 (1947).

[11] 333 U.S. 203 at 212 (1948).

[12] 343 U.S. 306 at 313 (1952).

[13] 374 U.S. 203 (1963).

[14] *Ibid.* at 222.

[15] 366 U.S. 420 at 442 (1961).

[16] 374 U.S. 203 at 265 (1963).

[17] 366 U.S. 420 at 462 (1961).

[18] The dissenting opinion in Everson v. Board of Education, 350 U.S. 1, at page 26 (1947) states concerning the First Amendment: "It was intended not only to keep the states' hands out of religion, but to keep religion's hand off the state, and above all, to keep bitter religious controversy from getting control

of public policy or the public purse." McGowan v. Maryland, 366 U.S. 420 at page 430 (1961) indicates that the "writings of Madison, who was the First Amendment's architect, demonstrate that the establishment of a religion was equally feared because of its tendencies to political tyranny and subversion of civil authority."

[19] 367 U.S. 488 at 495 (1961).

[20] Robert Hutchins, as quoted in *Christian Century*, Dec. 4, 1963, p. 1512.

[21] *Ibid.*

CHAPTER 2

[1] *Congressional Record*, May 11, 1954, p. 5999.

[2] Quoted by Peter Berger, *The Noise of Solemn Assemblies* (Garden City, N.Y., Doubleday, 1961), p. 63.

[3] For fuller discussion of the Becker Amendment see Chapter 6.

[4] "Relations Between Church and State," United Presbyterian Church, Witherspoon Building, Philadelphia.

[5] "Church and State, a Lutheran Perspective," Board of Social Ministry, Lutheran Church in America, 231 Madison Ave., New York, N.Y.

CHAPTER 3

[1] John A. Ryan and Francis J. Boland, *Catholic Principles of Politics* (New York: Macmillan, 1960), pp. 313, 314.

[2] *Ibid.*, pp. 319, 326–30.

[3] John Courtney Murray, S.J., "Governmental Repression of Heresy," *Proceedings of the Catholic Theological Society of America*, III (June, 1949), p. 90.

[4] John Courtney Murray, S.J., *Theological Studies* (New York: America Press), X, 223.

[5] W. L. Emerson, "The Religious Liberty Schema," *Liberty*, Jan.–Feb., 1966, p. 12.

[6] Michael P. Sheridan, S.J., "Students' Rights in Higher Education," *America*, May 21, 1966, pp. 731–32.

[7] *The New York Times*, June 14, 1965.

[8] *The New York Times*, June 15, 1965.

[9] *The New York Times*, June 24, 1965.

CHAPTER 4

[1] *United States Department of Commerce Statistical Abstract*, 1962, 83rd ed., pp. 46–48.

[2] *The Catholic Reporter* (diocesan newspaper), Aug. 3, 1962.

[3] *Ibid.*, April 3, 1964.

[4] Rabbi Arthur Gilbert, "The Mission of the Jewish People," lecture delivered at Lutheran World Federation Consultation on the Church and the Jewish People, Denmark, 1964 (New York: National Conference of Christians and Jews), p. 29.

[5] *Ibid.*, p. 31.

[6] Edwin E. Aubrey, *Secularism: A Myth* (New York: Harper, 1954), p. 119.

[7] 374 U.S. 203.

CHAPTER 5

[1] Lewis J. Sherrill, *Presbyterian Parochial Schools, 1841–1870* (New Haven: Yale University Press, 1932).

[2] Mary Perkins Ryan, *Are Parochial Schools the Answer?* (New York: Holt, Rinehart & Winston, 1964), pp. 33, 34.

[3] Denver *Post*, July 26, 1966.

[4] For discussion of dual school enrollment see Chapter 9.

[5] *The Catholic Reporter*, Jan. 24, 1964.

[6] W. T. Jones, *History of Western Philosophy* (New York: Harcourt Brace, 1952), p. 622.

[7] Emil Brunner, *Divine Imperative* (Philadelphia: Westminster Press, 1947), p. 511.

[8] St. Louis: Concordia Publishing House, 1961, p. 5.

[9] Richard Hamill, *Philosophy of Seventh-Day Adventist Education* (Washington, D.C.: General Conference of Seventh Day Adventists, 1959), p. 11.

[10] *The Catholic Reporter*, Sept. 13, 1963.

[11] Ryan, *op. cit.*, pp. 48–49.

[12] Rev. John M. Joyce, "Would Catholic Education Have Spoiled JFK?," *The Critic*, Oct.–Nov., 1964.

[13] *The Catholic Reporter*, Sept. 13, 1963.

[14] Ryan, *op. cit.*, p. 170.

[15] *The Catholic Reporter*, Feb. 28, 1964.

[16] *Ibid.*, Dec. 7, 1964.

CHAPTER 6

[1] *The Catholic Reporter*, June 21, 1963.

[2] *The New York Times*, May 1, 1964.

[3] Jules Cohen, "Religion in the Public Schools" (New York: National Women's League of United Synagogue of America, 1957).

[4] Leo Pfeffer, *Church, State and Freedom* (Boston: Beacon, 1953), p. 306.

[5] *Public School Sectarianism and the Jewish Child* (New York: American Jewish Congress), p. 10.

[6] Pfeffer, *op. cit*, p. 306.

[7] Dean M. Kelley, "Beyond Separation of Church and State," Department of Religious Liberty, National Council of Churches, undated.

CHAPTER 7

[1] John A. Ryan and Francis J. Boland, *Catholic Principles of Politics* (New York: Macmillan, 1960), pp. 141–42.

[2] Emil Brunner, *Justice and the Social Order* (New York: Harper, 1945), p. 111.

[3] Ryan and Boland, *op. cit.*, p. 142.

[4] Kansas City *Times*, July 29, 1963.

[5] *Ibid.*

[6] *Ibid.*

[7] *Ibid.*

[8] *Digest of Educational Statistics, 1964* (Washington: U.S. Department of Health, Education and Welfare), p. 18.

[9] Fred F. Beach, *The State and Non-Public Schools* (Washington: U.S. Department of Health, Education and Welfare, 1958), p. 2.

[10] *Digest of Educational Statistics, 1964*, *op. cit.*, pp. 18, 19, 24.

[11] Virgil Blum, " 'Freedom of Choice' in Schools," *U.S. News and World Report*, Oct. 25, 1957, p. 109.

[12] George R. LaNoue, "Public Funds for Parochial Schools" (New York: National Council of Churches, 1963), p. 22.

[13] CEF presentation to Kansas City, Mo., Board of Education, June 4, 1964.

[14] "Parents' Civil Rights in Education," undated leaflet published by CEF.

[15] Blum, *op. cit.*, p. 109.

CHAPTER 8

[1] Everson v. Board of Education of Township of Ewing, 330 U.S. 1 (1947).

[2] Gurney v. Ferguson, 190 Okla 254, 122 Pacific 2nd. 1002. Matthews v. Quinton, 362 P. 2nd. 932.

[3] See "Growth of Pupil Transportation in Missouri," Report of the Public Schools of the State of Missouri for School Year Ending June 30, 1963, pp. 17–20; and remarks of State Senator Graham S. Newell of Vermont during Senate debate, Mar. 16, 1955.

[4] Accident Statistics, 1963, National Safety Council.

[5] *The New York Times*, Aug. 7, 1965.

[6] R. L. Hunt, "Why Bus Transportation," *Phi Delta Kappan*, May, 1961.

[7] 374 U.S. 203 (1963), pp. 241–42.

CHAPTER 9

[1] Marvin J. Taylor, "Whither the Church's Education?," *Andover Newton Quarterly*, Sept., 1964, p. 23.

[2] "Shared Time: Answer to an Impasse," *Christianity and Crisis*, Sept. 19, 1961.

[3] "Shared Time: A Proposal for the Education of Children," *Religious Education*, Jan.–Feb., 1962, p. 5.

[4] *Proposed Federal Promotion of Shared Time*, U.S. Senate Subcommittee on Education, June 14, 1963, p. 1. Hereafter referred to as Senate Report.

[5] Brooklyn *Tablet*, Apr. 21, 1966.

[6] Leo Adolph, "Shared Time—A Threat to Public School," *Progressive World*, July, 1963, p. 17.

[7] Senate Report, p. 1.

[8] *Chicago Today*, Winter, 1965, Vol. IV, No. 1, p. 2, University of Chicago.

[9] See *The New York Times*, Jan. 2, 1965, p. 1.

[10] *Dual Enrollment in Public and Non-Public Schools*, U.S. Office of Education, OE 24014–1965. Hereafter referred to as *Dual Enrollment*.

[11] Religious News Service dispatch from Columbus, Nov. 2, 1965.

[12] Edward Wakin, "The Shared Time Experiment: How It Operates," *Saturday Review*, Feb. 15, 1964, p. 82.

[13] Louis Cassels, "A Way Out of Our Parochial-Public School Conflict," *Look*, Aug. 28, 1962, pp. 54–56.

[14] Senate Report, p. 10.

[15] House Committee on Education and Labor, *Hearings on Aid to Elementary and Secondary Education*, 89th Cong., 1st Sess., p. 841.

[16] *Ibid.*, p. 801.

[17] Testimony of Professor Carl Bangs of Saint Paul School of Theology, Kansas City, Mo., before Missouri Senate Education Committee, Mar. 15, 1966.

[18] Senate Report, p. 10.

[19] *Ibid.*

[20] *Dual Enrollment*, p. 7.

[21] *Ibid.*, p. 70.

[22] *Ibid.*, p. 7.

[23] *Ibid.*, p. 52.

[24] *Ibid.*, p. 60.

[25] Glenn Archer, "The Truth About Shared Time" (Washington, *Americans United For Separation of Church and State*, 1966) p. 21.

[26] Senate Report, p. 9.

[27] *Ibid.*, p. 8.

[28] *Dual Enrollment*, p. 80.

CHAPTER 10

[1] House Report 1814, 89th Cong., 2d Sess., 1966.

[2] Elementary and Secondary Education Act of 1965, Section 205 (a) (2).

[3] House Report 1814, *op. cit.*, pp. 4–5.

[4] Office of Education publication 20076, "A Description and Analysis of the Elementary and Secondary Education Act of 1965."

[5] Washington *Evening Star*, Jan. 22, 1965, p. 3A.

[6] Hearings on Aid to Elementary and Secondary Education, General Subcommittee on Education of the House Committee on Education and Labor, 89th Cong., 1st Sess., p. 812.

[7] *Ibid.*, p. 841.

[8] Adopted Feb. 26, 1965 by the General Board of the National Council of Churches, meeting at Portland, Oregon.

[9] *Proposed Federal Promotion of Shared Time*, U.S. Senate Committee on Harbor and Public Welfare Education, Report No. 146, 89th Cong., 1st Sess. (1965), p. 12.

[10] *Christian Century*, May 11, 1966, pp. 628–29.

[11] *Federal Register*, 30 F.R. 13138–13142, 118.11.

[12] *Christian Century*, May 11, 1966, p. 628.

[13] *Ibid.*

[14] Testimony by Dean Kelley for the National Council of Churches on extension of the Elementary and Secondary Education Act of 1965, Senate Subcommittee on Education, May 5, 1966.

[15] Board of Education v. Allen, 273 NYS 2nd 239.

[16] Testimony of Jesse Margolin before New York City Board of Education on resolution authorizing projects in nonpublic schools, 1966.

[17] *The Catholic News*, Apr. 28, 1966.

[18] *Ibid.*, Apr. 21, 1966.

[19] *The New York Times*, Aug. 18, 1966.

[20] House Report 1814, Part 2, 89th Cong., 2d Sess., 1966, p. 3.

[21] Aug., 1966, p. 2.

[22] "The Church/State Problem Has Been Handed on to You"—A Guide for Community Groups, American Civil Liberties Union, June, 1967.

CHAPTER 11

[1] Undated promotional brochure.

[2] Catalogue for 1965–66, p. 17.

[3] Catalogue for 1962–63.

[4] Catalogue for 1963–64.

[5] Catalogue for 1964–65, p. 20.

[6] *Bulletin*, 1963–65, p. 31.

[7] *Bulletin*, 1964–66, p. 27.

[8] Catalogue for 1962–63.

[9] Horace Mann League of the United States v. Board of Public Works of Maryland, 385 U.S. 97 (1966). The three colleges were Western Maryland, which is Methodist, Notre Dame and St. Joseph College, both Roman Catholic.

[10] Hood College.

[11] Edward Wakin, "How Catholic Is a Catholic College?" *Saturday Review*, Apr. 16, 1966, p. 92.

[12] *Ibid.*, p. 93.

[13] *Ibid.*, p. 94.

[14] Wakin, *op. cit.*, p. 105.

CHAPTER 12

1 Public Law 81–475, sec. 401 *et. seq;* 12 U.S.C. 1749.
2 Public Law 85–864; sec. 201 *et. seq;* P.L. 87–344; P.L. 88–665; 20 U.S.C. 421 *et seq.*
3 Public Law 85–864, sec. 401 *et seq;* P.L. 87–344; P.L. 88–665; 20 U.S.C. 464.
4 Alice Moody, "Survey of Government Programs Related to or in Some Measure Implemented Through Church-related Agencies and Institutions," Baptist Joint Committee on Public Affairs, 1965.
5 Public Law 88–204, sec. 202 *et. seq.*
6 Moody, *op. cit.*
7 Public Law 88–204, sec. 301 *et. seq.*
8 Public Law 81–152, as amended, sec. 203(j) and 203(k); 42 U.S.C. 484 (j) and (k).
9 Public Law 89–10, Title IV.
10 Richard Selleck, "The Church and Higher Education," *Michigan Christian Advocate,* Sept. 29, 1966, p. 8.
11 Moody, *op. cit.*
12 John M. Swomley, Jr., *The Military Establishment* (Boston: Beacon, 1964) pp. 214–15.
13 House hearings on Defense Department appropriations for 1963, Part 5, pp. 81, 84.
14 *The New York Times,* May 25, 1965.

CHAPTER 13

1 State v. Garber, 419 P. 2nd 896; 197 Kansas 567 November 5, 1966; certiorari denied 389 US 51, 88 S. Ct. 236, 19L Ed. 2d 50.
2 G.S. 1901, Par. 6420.
3 "Do We Believe in Religious Liberty for the Amish?," National Committee for Amish Religious Freedom, Farmers State Bank, Yoder, Kansas.
4 Des Moines *Register,* Apr. 16, 1967, p. 6G.
5 *Ibid.,* July 1, 1967.
6 98 U.S. 145, 25 L. Ed. 244.
7 310 U.S. 624.

CHAPTER 14

1 Rabbi Arthur Hertzberg, "Church, State, and the Jews," *Commentary,* Dec. 1962.
2 John Courtney Murray, S.J., *We Holds These Truths* (New York: Sheed & Ward, 1960).
3 *The Sacred Canons* (St. Louis, Herder, 1957), II, 611.
4 *Catholic Reporter,* diocesan newspaper, Kansas City–St. Joseph, Mar. 12, 1965.
5 *Ibid.,* May 8, 1964.
6 New York *Post,* June 19, 1967.
7 *The New York Times,* Aug. 17, 1967.
8 Kansas City *Star,* Mar. 16, 1961.

CONCLUSION

1 Peter H. and Alice S. Rossi, "Some Effects of Parochial School Education in America," *Daedalus,* Spring, 1961, p. 325.
2 *Ibid.*
3 *Ibid.,* p. 326.

Appendix

MAJOR SUPREME COURT DECISIONS
AFFECTING CHURCH, STATE AND EDUCATION

Date	Case	Decision	Vote
1908	Quick Bear v. Leupp 210 U.S. 50	The federal government could disburse funds, held in trust for the Indians, to church schools so designated by the Indians to be used for tuition purposes. The government was simply holding funds in trust, not using government funds for church schools.	9–0
1925	Pierce v. Society of Sisters of the Holy Names of Jesus and Mary 268 U.S. 510	Oregon's Compulsory Education Act of 1922 requiring public school attendance of all children 8 to 16 years of age was held unconstitutional, not on Church–State grounds but for its restraint on business or commerce, in this case private religious schools.	9–0

1930	Cochran v. Louisiana State Board of Education 281 U.S. 370	A state law providing for furnishing of secular textbooks to public and nonpublic (parochial) school children was held constitutional but not on First Amendment grounds. The textbook benefits were given "to the children," not to the schools as such.	8–0
1943	West Virginia State Board of Education vs. Barnette 310 U.S. 624	The state's compulsory flag salute law previously upheld in Minersville (Pa.) School District v. Gobitis (310 U.S. 586, 1940) was declared unconstitutional. "No official . . . can prescribe what shall be orthodox in politics, nationalism, religion, or other matters of opinion, or force citizens to confess by word or act their faith therein."	6–3
1947	Everson v. Board of Education of Ewing Township, N.J. 330 U.S. 1	Court upheld right of a state to provide for reimbursing parents of public and private school pupils for bus transportation to such schools.	5–4
1948	Illinois *ex. rel.* McCollum v. Board of Education 333 U.S. 203	"Released time" programs on public school property under compulsory attendance provisions and machinery was judged unconstitutional in violation of First Amendment.	8–1
1952	Zorach v. Clauson 343 U.S. 306	"Released time" programs where religion classes were held away from public school property for those who wanted to attend was held constitutional, even though other pupils continued their classes in the public schools.	6–3
1962	Engel v. Vitale 370 U.S. 421	A 22-word nondenominational prayer prepared and administered by public officials was held unconstitutional. ". . . government in this country should stay out of the business of writing or sanctioning official prayers. . . ."	8–1

| 1963 | Abington School District v. Schempp and Murray v. Curlett
374 U.S. 203 | A Pennsylvania requirement of Bible reading and Maryland's practice of both Bible reading and recitation of the Lord's Prayer in public schools were held to violate the establishment clause of the First Amendment. The "concept of neutrality" to which our government is committed on religious matters "does not permit a State to require a religious exercise even with the consent of the majority of those affected. . . ." | 8–1 |

The decisions of at least three state courts should be noted. They were allowed to stand when the Supreme Court refused to review or denied *certiorari.*

1. Anderson v. Swart, 366 U.S. 925 (1961): a Vermont Supreme Court decision held unconstitutional the use, by a school district with no high school, of public funds for tuition for children attending a private (parochial) school in a neighboring town.
2. Dickman v. School District, Oregon City, 371 U.S. 823 (1962): Oregon's Supreme Court, in a 6–1 decision, held that school districts must stop providing free textbooks to parochial schools even though the textbooks were secular and only loaned to pupils.
3. Board of Public Works of Maryland v. Horace Mann League of U.S., 385 U.S. 97 (1966): a Court of Appeals of Maryland decision held unconstitutional state grants for construction of buildings to two Roman Catholic and one Methodist college, while permitting a similar grant to another college regarded as "essentially secular."

Bibliography

ABRAHAM, HENRY J. *Freedom and the Court.* New York: Oxford University Press, 1967.

ABBOTT, WALTER M., S.J. (ed.). *The Documents of Vatican II.* New York: Association Press, 1966.

American Association of School Administrators. *Religion in the Public Schools.* New York: Harper & Row, 1964.

ANTIEAU, CHESTER JAMES, PHILLIP MARK CARROLL and THOMAS CARROLL BURKE. *Religion Under the State Constitutions.* New York: Central Book, 1965.

———. *Freedom from Federal Establishment.* Milwaukee: Bruce, 1964.

Association of Council Secretaries. *Relations Between Church and State.* Boston: Massachusetts Council of Churches, 1960.

AUBREY, EDWIN C. *Secularism: A Myth.* New York: Harper, 1954.

BAINTON, ROLAND. *The Travail of Religious Liberty.* New York: Harper, 1961.

Baptist Joint Committee on Public Affairs, Religious Liberty Conferences: Study Papers on "Church–State Relations in Higher Education," 1962.

BATES, M. SEARLE. *Religious Liberty: An Inquiry.* New York: International Missionary Council, 1945.

BEACH, FRED F. *The State and Non-Public Schools.* Washington: U.S. Department of Health, Education and Welfare, 1958.

BENNETT, JOHN C. *Christians and the State.* New York: Scribner's, 1958.

BERGER, PETER L. *The Noise of Solemn Assemblies.* Garden City, N.Y.: Doubleday, 1961.

BLANSHARD, PAUL. *American Freedom and Catholic Power.* Boston: Beacon, 1958.

——. *Religion and the Schools: The Great Controversy.* Boston: Beacon, 1963.

BLUM, VIRGIL, S. J. *Freedom of Choice in Education.* New York: Macmillan, 1958.

BOLES, DONALD E. *The Bible, Religion and the Public Schools.* Ames, Iowa: Iowa State University Press, 1961.

BRICKMAN, WILLIAM W. and STANLEY LEHRER. *Religion, Government and Education.* New York: Society for the Advancement of Education, 1961.

BRUNNER, EMIL *The Divine Imperative,* Philadelphia: Westminster, 1947.

BUTTS, R. FREEMAN. *The American Tradition in Religion and Education.* Boston: Beacon, 1950.

CALLAHAN, DANIEL (ed.). *Federal Aid and Catholic Schools.* Baltimore: Helicon, 1964.

CARRILLO DE ALBORNOZ, A. F. *The Basis of Religious Liberty.* New York: Association Press, 1963.

——. *Roman Catholicism and Religious Liberty.* Geneva: World Council of Churches, 1959.

"The Church–State Problem Has Been Handed on to You." New York: American Civil Liberties Union, 1967.

COGLEY, JOHN (ed.). *Religion in America.* New York: Meridian, 1958.

CULLMAN, OSCAR. *The State in the New Testament.* New York: Scribner's, 1956.

CUNINGGIM, MERRIMON. *Freedom's Holy Light.* New York: Harper's, 1955.

DIERENFIELD, RICHARD B. *Religion in American Public Schools.* Washington: Public Affairs Press, 1962.

DOERRIES, HERMANN. *Constantine and Religious Liberty.* New Haven: Yale University Press, 1960.

DOUGLAS, WILLIAM O. *The Bible and the Schools.* Boston: Little, Brown, 1966.

DRINAN, ROBERT F. *Religion, the Courts, and Public Policy.* New York: McGraw–Hill, 1963.

Dual Enrollment in Public and Non-Public Schools. Washington: U.S. Office of Education, 1965.

EDWARDS, NEWTON. *The Courts and the Public Schools.* Chicago: University of Chicago Press, 1955.

FREUND, PAUL A. and ROBERT ULICH. *Religion and the Public School: The Legal Issue—The Educational Issue.* Cambridge: Harvard University Press, 1965.

FROMMER, ARTHUR (ed.). *The Bible and the Public Schools.* New York: Affiliated Publishers, 1963.

GORDIS, ROBERT, et al. Religion and the Schools. Santa Barbara: Fund for the Republic, 1959.

HAMILL, RICHARD. "Philosophy of Seventh Day Adventist Education." Washington: General Conference of Seventh Day Adventists, 1959.

HEALEY, ROBERT M. Jefferson on Religion in Public Education. New Haven: Yale University Press, 1962.

HOWE, MARK. The Garden and the Wilderness. Chicago: University of Chicago Press, 1965.

HUEGLI, ALBERT G. Church and State Under God. St. Louis: Concordia, 1964.

———— (ed.). God's Right and Left Hands. St. Louis: Concordia, 1964.

JOHNSON, ALVIN W. and FRANK H. YOST. Separation of Church and State in the U.S. Minneapolis: University of Minnesota Press, 1948.

A Journal of Church and State. Ed. by James E. Wood, Jr. Published quarterly by J. M. Dawson Studies in Church and State of Baylor University, Waco, Texas. 1958.

KATZ, WILBER G. Religion and American Constitutions. Evanston: Northwestern University Press, 1964.

KAUPER, PAUL. Civil Liberties and the Constitution. Ann Arbor: University of Michigan Press, 1962.

————. Religion and the Constitution. Baton Rouge: Louisiana State University Press, 1964.

KERWIN, JEROME G. Catholic Viewpoint on Church and State. Garden City, N.Y.: Hanover House, 1960.

KURLAND, PHILIP B. "Of Church and State and the Supreme Court." Chicago: University of Chicago Law School, 1961.

————. Religion and the Law. Chicago: Aldine Publishing Co., 1962.

LANOUE, GEORGE R. "Public Funds for Parochial Schools?" New York: National Council of Churches, 1963.

LEE, JAMES MICHAEL (ed.). Catholic Education in the Western World. Notre Dame: University of Notre Dame Press, 1967.

LITTELL, FRANKLIN H. From State Church to Pluralism. Garden City, N.Y.: Doubleday, 1962.

————. The Free Church. Boston: Starr King Press, 1956.

LODER, JAMES E. Religion and the Public Schools. New York: Association Press, 1965.

LOVE, THOMAS T. John Courtney Murray: Contemporary Church–State Theory. Garden City, New York: Doubleday, 1965.

Lutheran Church in America, Board of Social Ministry. "Church and State, a Lutheran Perspective." New York.

MANWARING, DAVID R. Render Unto Caesar. Chicago: University of Chicago Press, 1962.

MARTY, MARTIN, JOSEPH MOODY, and ARTHUR HERZBERG. The Outbursts That Await Us. New York: Macmillan, 1963.

MCCOLLUM, VASHTI. One Woman's Fight, 1951–1961. Boston: Beacon, 1961.

McCluskey, Neil G., S.J. *Catholic Viewpoint on Education.* Garden City, N.Y.: Doubleday, 1959.

———. *Public Schools and Moral Education: The Influence of Horace Mann, William Torrey Harris and John Dewey.* New York: Columbia University Press, 1958.

McGrath, John J. *Church and State in American Law.* Milwaukee: Bruce, 1962.

McLoughlin, Emmett. *American Culture and Catholic Schools.* New York: Lyle Stuart, 1960.

Moehlman, Conrad H. *The Wall of Separation Between Church and State.* Boston: Beacon Press, 1951.

National Catholic Welfare Conference, "The Constitutionality of the Inclusion of Church-Related Schools in Federal Aid to Education." Washington, D.C. National Catholic Welfare Conference Legal Department, 1961.

Nichols, Roy F. *Religion and American Democracy.* Baton Rouge: Louisiana State University Press, 1959.

Oaks, Dollin H. *The Wall Between Church and State.* Chicago: University of Chicago Press, 1963.

Powell, Theodore. *The School Bus Law.* Middletown, Conn.: Wesleyan University Press, 1960.

Pfeffer, Leo. *Creeds in Competition.* New York: Harper, 1958.

———. *Church, State, and Freedom.* Boston: Beacon, 1966.

"Public School Sectarianism and the Jewish Child." New York: American Jewish Congress.

Religion and the Public Order: An Annual Review of Church and State and of Religion, Law and Society, Villanova University School of Law. Ed. by Donald A. Giannelli. Chicago: University of Chicago Press. 1964.

Rice, Charles E. *The Supreme Court and Public Prayer.* New York: Fordham University Press, 1964.

Ryan, Rev. John A., and Boland, Francis J. *Catholic Principles of Politics: The State and the Church.* New York: Macmillan, 1960.

Ryan, Mary Perkins. *Are Parochial Schools the Answer?* New York: Holt, Rinehart & Winston, 1964.

Sanders, Thomas G. *Protestant Concepts of Church and State.* New York: Holt, Rinehart & Winston, 1964.

Sherrill, Lewis J. *Presbyterian Parochial Schools.* New Haven: Yale University Press, 1932.

Smith, Elwyn A. *Church and State in Your Community.* Philadelphia: Westminster Press, 1963.

Stokes, Anson Phelps. *Church and State in the United States.* New York: Harper, 1950.

Stokes, Anson Phelps, and Leo Pfeffer. *Church and State in the United States.* New York: Harper & Row, 1964.

Thayer, V. T. *The Attack on the American Secular School.* Boston: Beacon, 1951.

TIERNEY, BRIAN. *The Crisis of Church and State 1050–1300*. Englewood Cliffs, N.J.: Prentice–Hall, 1964.

TUSSMAN, JOSEPH (ed.). *The Supreme Court on Church and State*. New York: Oxford University Press, 1961.

United Presbyterian Church in the U.S.A. *Relations Between Church and State*. Adopted by the 175th General Assembly, Philadelphia, May, 1963.

Villanova Law School's Institute of Church and State:

Proceedings, Vol. II, "Private Trusts and Public Law" and "Private Schools and Public Law," 1959.

Proceedings, Vol. III, "Secularism and Religious Freedom" and Vol. IV, "Law and Religious Pluralism," 1963.

WALTER, ERICH A. *Religion and the State University*. Ann Arbor: University of Michigan Press, 1958.

WOGAMAN, PHILIP. *Protestant Faith and Religious Liberty*. New York: Abingdon, 1967.

Index